JAN -- 2014

JAN -- 2014

At Home in New England

At Home in New England

ROYAL BARRY WILLS ARCHITECTS

1925 TO PRESENT

Richard Wills *with Keith Orlesky*

ROWMAN &
LITTLEFIELD

Lanham • Boulder • New York • Toronto • Plymouth, UK

Contents

Acknowledgments 7

Authors' Note 7

Introduction 9

The Style of "Home" 13

The Legacy of Royal Barry Wills 21

Houses 31

Notes 191

Image Credits 191

Acknowledgments

After eighty years in business the responsibilities for any endeavor at the firm cannot be credited to a single person. The spirit of Royal Barry Wills has been carried forward principally by his son, Richard Wills, who has designed the majority of homes and buildings featured in this volume. The authorship of this particular work is the result of a collaboration of all members of the firm past and present, including G. Alexander Domenico, Todd Fix, Douglas Lipscomb, Robert Pesiri, AnnMarie Squadrito, David Stuhlsatz, Lynn Talacko, and Jessica Barry Wills.

We owe Keith Orlesky a debt of gratitude for the descriptive captions and the text that introduces our work.

Authors' Note

Most of the houses showcased here represent work done by the firm in the last decade. We have also selected some homes featured in our previous book *Houses for Good Living* that date back more than forty years. Their inclusion demonstrates our conviction that good design has timeless qualities that can be appreciated by any generation.

Introduction

To be happy at home is the ultimate result of all ambition, the end to which every enterprise and labour tends, and of which every desire prompts the execution.

—Samuel Johnson, *The Rambler*, no. 68,
Saturday, November 10, 1750

There is, of course, a degree of irony in the need for any sort of introduction to the work of Royal Barry Wills Associates. It is, after all, one of the country's most venerable firms and was led by, certainly in the mid-twentieth century, one of its most well-known architects. And the houses it has and continues to produce, many of which are celebrated in this volume, are quintessential examples of the best qualities we associate with New England architecture. Quiet, confident, and unselfconscious, they are as remarkable for their artistic and qualitative consistency as they are for the ease with which they sit within their surroundings. Even a casual, uneducated examination of these buildings is rewarded by the attention that has been paid to proportion, composition, detail, aspect, and setting in their construction. In a time when seemingly nothing but size matters, the houses shown here remind us of what can be achieved when skilled hands are guided by keen, practiced, and benevolent eyes. Where, then, does the restraint and refinement in these buildings come from?

Clearly there is tradition at work here, but it is not just the way the buildings reflect and interpret the time-honored building methods and styles that we associate with New England. This is the work of a firm that has its own traditions, refined in almost ninety years of practice, devoted almost exclusively to the simple proposition of building comfortable, attractive, and practical homes for American families. If ever we have attempted, whether from passion or envy, to create something of quality, we quickly learn that making something look easy is anything but. The defining characteristic of these houses is exactly that quality of unstudied, seemingly effortless elegance that only long and conscientious practice can provide.

The path to this level of sophistication and achievement was improbable at best. It began in 1925 when a marine engineer not long graduated from the Massachusetts Institute of Technology took the bold initiative to set up his own one-man architecture practice in a small rented space in Boston. The aspiring architect, with the imposing sobriquet Royal Barry Wills, was thirty years old and could claim only six years as a design engineer with the Turner Construction Company as his principal professional credential. Unlike many of his contemporaries, his interest in design was and would remain almost solely confined to the small, middle- to upper-middle-class single-family house. Somehow, and in spite of the narrow margins inherent in his field of choice, a great depression, a world war, and a modernist revolution that threatened to dismiss every principle upon which his work was based, this determined, resourceful, and good-humored entrepreneur came to be one of America's most popular architects and, certainly, with sales of well over 500,000 books, its most popular architectural author.

Royal's son Richard Wills, the current firm's managing partner since 1965, began working with his father in 1952 while an architecture student attending the Boston Architectural Center. But his true legacy began when his father died in 1962, forcing Richard and longtime associates Merton Barrows, Robert Minot, and Warren Rohter to begin writing a new chapter in the firm's history.

It is hard to fathom the ways Richard has seen times and tastes, and with them the demands on the architect, change over the intervening fifty years. Competition for architectural services from designers, developers, homebuilders, and contractors on the one hand, and on the other the constraints of increasing professional liability, land and construction costs, and the loss of a shared sense of what looks "right" have all conspired to make today's client for traditional architectural services wealthier than those of the past, with an often corresponding increase in demand for space. It is no surprise, then, that along with new uses like media and family rooms and the expansion of some old ones, such as the number of bathrooms and cars, to accommodate that the typical Wills Associates house has grown in size over time. But to the consternation of many a modernist architect who has ascribed a physical prescription to the phrase "form follows function," the traditional Cape Cod home has proven remarkably adaptable to all the demands twenty-first-century lifestyles can throw at it. Far from being period recreations, the houses illustrated here are celebrations of this evolutionary quality of New England architecture. If there is any secret to the continued currency of the Royal Barry Wills Associates house it lies here, and in the persistent resonance that notion has with the people who are so happy to commission it. In that regard nothing much has changed since Merton Barrows summed up the firm's philosophy in a 1958 feature article in the *Saturday Evening Post*. "The best description of our stock in trade is domesticity. . . . We do an occasional contemporary home to satisfy clients who find domesticity in strictly functional surroundings. We prefer to fit modern concepts into traditional forms, simply because most of the people we deal with are at home in such a house."[1]

The Style of "Home"

Tradition is like a river that flows toward new ground.

—Wu Guanzhong

Strolling down the aisles of your typical local DIY superstore it's easy to forget that arrayed before you are virtually all of the thousands of pieces that go into the making of a typical new house in America. Lumber studs for walls and joists for floors and ceilings; doors; windows; trim and moldings; baseboards; door knobs; cupboards; countertops; wall, floor, and roof sheathing; lights and switches; plumbing pipes; insulation; wiring; sinks, toilets, bathtubs, faucets, and mirrors; hinges; shingles; and tile, just to name some of the obvious ones. And all the tools and finishing materials you'd need—from the hammers and tape measures to saws, drills, and portable power generators, nails, screws, adhesives, paint, wallpaper, carpet—are there, too. Equipped with several semitrailer trucks and considerably more ambition than what you were able to muster for painting the guest room, you could get all of it out the door with a credit card and a promise to pay later.

Of course, very few of us ever contemplate, much less undertake, such an exercise. A small number go the next closest step, giving that responsibility to an architect and his or her agent, the custom builder. For most homeowners, though, the components are only ever seen when they have already been selected and assembled into something we can walk through, a finished house. And after deciding where we'd like to live, how much space we think we need, and how much we can afford, the biggest choice left to us is what we want our home to look like. It is a credit to the cleverness of both builder and designer that the same materials can and have been combined into a dizzying array of combinations. Change things like the shape and slope of the roof; ceiling heights; the size, number, and location of windows (what architects call the fenestration pattern); the exterior materials; the amount and character of any decorative embellishment; the addition of a dormer or a porch, and then adjust the proportional relationship of these pieces to one another and you can get, well, almost anything you can imagine.

Intellectual prerogatives aside, and (mercifully) free of a bank assessor's opinion on resale value, the question confronting some of the earliest homebuilders in America, the settlers of the Cape area in Massachusetts almost four hundred years ago, was what to build if you had

to make every single piece of the house yourself—and if you had nothing but an axe, a handsaw, and a hammer with which to turn raw trees into shelter? The cottages at the modern reenactment village of Plimoth Plantation give us some clues and a vivid (if somewhat manicured) look into that moment in the past.

The European settlers who built the remarkably adroit structures upon which these recreations are based did so under the most trying conditions. Looking at a hand-hewn ceiling beam or a hand-split siding board we are reminded of the handiwork of people working not to the dictates of some stylistic convention, but rather to the deeply practical, relentless, and inescapable pressure of having too much to do in too little time. For preparing for the New World's unimaginably savage winters meant not just building shelter, but provisioning it, too. Creating arable land, growing or gathering crops, raising and tending livestock,

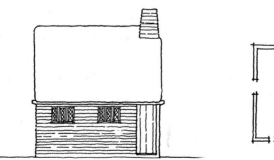 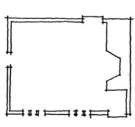 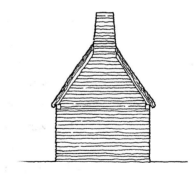

Plimoth Plantation Cottage

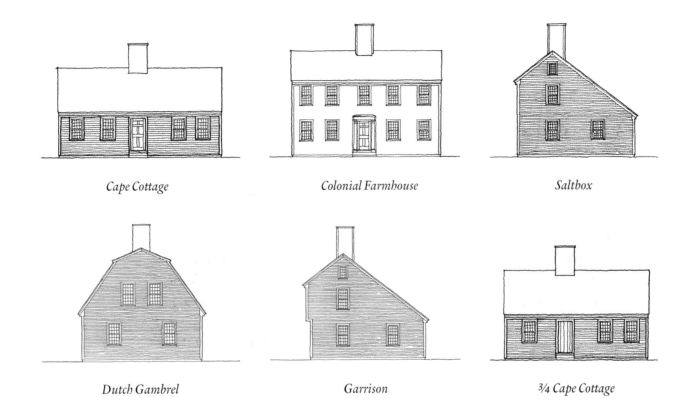

Cape Cottage

Colonial Farmhouse

Saltbox

Dutch Gambrel

Garrison

¾ Cape Cottage

childrearing, exploration, and self-defense all competed for the attention of the housebuilder. With the work required to create every stick of lumber and heat available only from a fireplace, it was no wonder that the earliest Colonial houses adopted the look of a child's drawing, the logical and unoriginal result of anyone making the next step in shelter beyond the rudiments of a tent or lean-to. Most were minimally sized one-room plans about the size of a modern-day dining room laid out as a simple square or compact rectangle, and which incorporated a storage loft beneath their steeply pitched roofs. They had no ornamental embellishments and but few small, crude windows.

In the next 150 years leading up to the Declaration of Independence, the European and New World–born population in America increased dramatically, moving south and west from the first settlements in New England and Virginia to the Ohio and Mississippi River Valleys and the Gulf Coast. Pride of place, prosperity, and confidence were all reflected in home and community building that was increasingly ambitious. Not surprisingly, the houses built in these new communities reflected their varied locations as well as the traditions and inclinations the settlers brought with them. In New England, the styles were many and varied and included the Cape cottage and its two-story cousin the Colonial

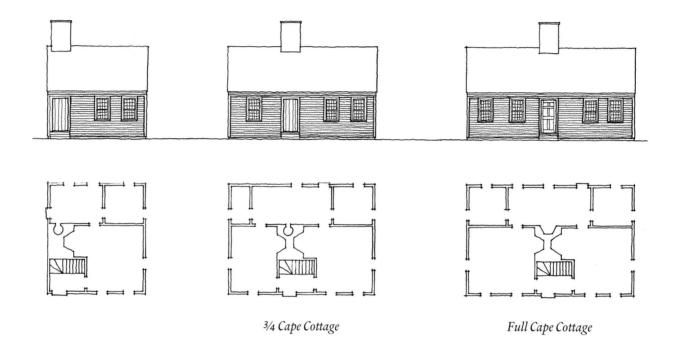

¾ Cape Cottage   *Full Cape Cottage*

farmhouse, as well as the saltbox, the garrison, the Dutch gambrel, and the three-quarter Cape, all of which appeared more or less concurrently in the seventeenth century. That despite their superficial differences they together appear distinctly New England to us is owed in part to the simplicity of their form—a centralized rectangular box more or less organized around a large central chimney—and in part because they retain, in the simplicity of their shape and detail, some of the essential DNA of their Colonial forebears.

The Cape is perhaps the most recognized of these many styles, and as erected by the first colonists it has a simple, rectangular floor plan with two or three rooms on the ground floor. This increase in size on the lower level made it possible for the second level to include living as well as storage space. Aside from wood siding (shingles or clapboards), its distinguishing features include its steeply pitched roof, a large central chimney, and an extraordinarily steep and narrow staircase. The front door is located, depending on the floor plan, in the center or just off center of the long side of the rectangle and faces the front of the property. Ceilings are low, often no more than seven feet, in no small part to control the amount of space that could be effectively heated in the winter. While the earliest windows were probably casement style that opened outward, the early adoption of the double-hung window became a defining and unifying aspect of all Colonial architecture.

The farmhouse style is more or less an extension of the Cape form, but with considerably more variation in the floor plan, in keeping with the many functional requirements of a farm building. Success in the farming enterprise brought with it the need to accommodate livestock, feed and wagons, ploughs and tools, and dairies, among other things, and which over time gave the New England farmhouse its compositional eccentricity and charm.

The two-story homes that most closely resemble a Cape tend to have a large central chimney and three or four rooms on the ground floor and four bedrooms upstairs. They often grew from one-half to full to saltbox. Staircases are similarly steep and narrow, typically squeezed into the space between the front door and the massive column of the chimney.

Colonial Farmhouse

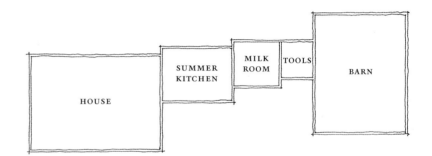

Evolution of the Saltbox House

Stylistic embellishment and the level of detail in carpentry—such as in moldings, cornices, pediments, and columns—appear haphazardly on the houses in direct proportion to the fortunes of the homeowner. Fashionable flourishes like flattened Greek temple fronts, raised paneling on walls, and crown molding were inspired then, as they are today, by the habits and tastes of the upper classes. These trends were widely circulated through illustrations in the many imported design treatises and architectural pattern books that were increasingly available, and through the considerable skill and direct experience European-born craftsmen brought with them.

By 1780 the Revolutionary War had been fought and won, the Colonial period in America had come to an end, and the new, emergent democracy had begun its long gestation toward its ultimate form on the world stage. Flushed with its hard-won success over its European masters and at the same time embarrassed by the crudeness of its origins, America rejected its colonial past and the buildings that had sheltered it. Largely forgotten in the rush to build a nation and dismissed as crude and rudimentary in comparison to the European precedents upon which so many of them were derived, the original Colonial house, in all its varied forms, almost vanished from the American landscape. For the remainder of the eighteenth century, America instead found expression for the seriousness of its newfound purpose in classical derivations of European-based styles such as Georgian and Queen Anne, Adamesque, and William and Mary. But it was not long into the Victorian age of the

Entrance & Fireplace Embellishments

nineteenth century that, again following a European lead, the lessons of more recent history began to receive recognition and command respect. A concerted effort to develop and, if necessary, invent a historical identity, a nascent interest in the preservation of a poorly documented past, the desire to create a genuinely American style, and most importantly a growing reverence for the near-mythical virtues of the Colonial pioneers and nation builders, all contributed to the creation of "the United States's most popular and characteristic expression,"[2] the Colonial Revival.

Despite the neglect of its early heritage, there yet existed a considerable amount of source material in New England to inspire and fuel such a revival, and by the first quarter of the twentieth century it had already been under way there for almost a hundred years. But its ascension to becoming the national style would depend on a number of complementary factors and coincidences, not the least of which was the emergence of a Boston architect named Royal Barry Wills.

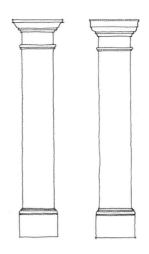

Doric Columns

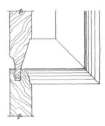

Raised Panel Detail

Crown Molding Details

Georgian   *Adams*

The Legacy of Royal Barry Wills

The Colonial Revival is the United States's most popular and characteristic expression.

—Richard Guy Wilson, *The Colonial Revival House*

The sampling of the work of Royal Barry Wills Associates that is included in this volume has, for the most part, been designed by Richard Wills, Royal Barry Wills's youngest son. The success of Richard's practice, noteworthy for its longevity as well as for its singular focus on the design of single-family homes, is evidenced by the houses on these pages and by the number of commissions he has and continues to attract. This work is, of course, a testament to his talent and that of his associates. But like most such stories, to an individual's talents, wit, and guile one must also acknowledge those elements of fortunate circumstance that can provide inspiration and crucial early advantage. And in Richard's case, one need look no further than the springboard his father's tutelage and fame provided.

At the height of his popularity, from the mid-1930s through the 1950s, Royal Barry Wills was literally a household name across the country, and it is by no means an exaggeration to say that he was among the most famous of any of America's architects of that period. Decorated by President Hoover for his design skills, proclaimed by the editors of *Life* magazine as the nation's most popular architectural author, featured constantly not only in all of the country's leading shelter magazines of the day but also in popular national gazettes like *Life* and *Parade* magazines, Wills was a national phenomenon—an inexplicably ubiquitous brand in a profession that wouldn't allow advertising by its members—practicing in a traditional style that was almost ignored by every academic and architecture school of his time. Houses he designed for the 1932 Boston Home Show, for the 1937 *Ladies' Home Journal* "Home of Tomorrow" exhibition in Madison Square Garden, and for the Western Pine Association at the 1939 Golden Gate Exposition in San Francisco were seen and walked through by hundreds of thousands of people. He designed literally thousands of homes across the country and influenced through his books and articles perhaps millions more, leaving a legacy of excellent design not just in those buildings, but also in the thriving successor firm he placed in the hands of his son and trusted associates. Most unusually for an architect, this success came exclusively on the basis of his design of traditional-looking houses, the vast majority of which were both small and intended for the American middle- and upper-middle-class market. So ubiquitous was his voice in the championing of the virtues of the qualities of the traditional New England vernacular architecture that "many a would-be homeowner, surveying the infinite variations of Mr. Wills Cape Codders in plan books and magazines, has concluded that he is the man who somehow invented the design."[3]

He had, of course, by no means invented it, but he became enamored of and an exponent of its virtues at exactly the right moment in American history. Born on August 21, 1895, in Melrose, Massachusetts, his professional life began when he entered the MIT engineering school, graduating in 1918 as an architectural engineer. It was perhaps the first demonstration of the practical aspect of his proudly held New England heritage, one he would maintain throughout his professional life. After a tour in the navy and subsequent employment at a shipyard, he found work as a draftsman and design engineer with the Turner Construction Company in Boston. But it was not long before his artistic bent and am-

bition led him down a more singular path. He had noticed an occasional house plan published on the real-estate page of one of the local papers and his offer to supply better plans, for free, was accepted. After several of his plans had appeared, a few venturesome clients sought him out at the offices of the construction firm. In an interview with Arnold Nicholson in the 1958 issue of the *Saturday Evening Post* titled "Big Man in Small Houses," he described the results:

> *"I arranged to have them call when the brass was out of town," he told me, "and held our consultations in the plush office of the president. This worked for quite a while, but as my clientele grew, it became a real strain on my ingenuity and the tolerance of the company. I beat the president to the draw and quit to set up my own shop."*[4]

Thus set up in a one-room office in a building on lower Beacon Street in 1925, Wills kept busy with a series of increasingly comprehensive commissions. His early work was eclectic and often in European-inspired period revival styles then in vogue. But increasingly his attention and reputation became focused on designs based on the regional New England vernacular, in particular the Cape Cod cottage. The 1928 remodeling and restoration of the early-nineteenth-century Charles G. Eichenberger house in Egypt, Massachusetts, was his first widely published Cape Cod design.[5] In it we can begin to see the hallmarks of Wills's later success: a very discerning eye that understood and could sympathetically expand on the purity of the abstracted Cape Cod cottage form, his knack for getting his work published, and a sincere interest in the needs of his clients and the ways that their changing lifestyles could and should be reflected in the layout of the houses they chose for themselves.

Wills's transition from a locally respected practitioner to a national voice began as the result of indirect support from an unexpected and unwitting source. Herbert Hoover, himself trained as an engineer, served two terms as secretary of commerce under Republican presidents Warren Harding and Calvin Coolidge. As early as 1921 he had established a Division of Building and Housing in the Commerce Department in an attempt to maximize mass consumption and add impetus to a sputtering economy. As the country ground into the Depression at the end of that decade, Hoover supported a variety of ideas that built on that principle, but with a particular focus on ways to make the small, affordable house attractive to American consumers. One such idea was federal government support and sponsorship of the National Better Homes Competition. In 1929 Wills won a First Regional Prize, and followed that with a National Gold Medal in 1932, and silver and bronze medals in the competitions of 1934 and 1935. Wills built on this success, and between 1935 and 1942 he entered and won two dozen competitions, including those sponsored by *Pencil Points*, *House Beautiful*, *Better Homes and Gardens*, and *Ladies' Home Journal*.[6]

Wills's participation in competitions at this time was, of course, partly brought about by the time he had on his hands as the result of a lack of paying commissions, but it was also an integral component of a theory he was developing, about how one could make a living in the decidedly risky proposition of architecture in general and the even more precarious business of designing houses. As early as 1931 he outlined "his pragmatic, realistic approach to architectural practice in 'The Successful Business of Small House Architecture,' which he published in *Architectural Forum*."[7] Wills refined his arguments and then consolidated them in a best-selling book in 1941, *This Business of Architecture*. Although the drafting-room organizational suggestions he makes may seem dated to today's computerized professionals, the principles espoused in the book and the lessons it presents remain relevant. Wills addresses head on some of the key issues facing a fractured, poorly organized professional organization of architects at that time, in particular their prohibition of advertising, and therefore the thorny problem of how one would go about getting work. His approach was direct and lighthearted, benefitting from the author's characteristic good humor and his gift for drawing. Wills had combined these traits as a cartoonist while a student at MIT, and they served him well as he illustrated the direct and indirect ways one could chase that illusive prey, the paying client.[8] "You want people who are going to build to desire your service . . . , some of them have prejudices that are soluble in a bath of simple, authoritative, persistent education."[9]

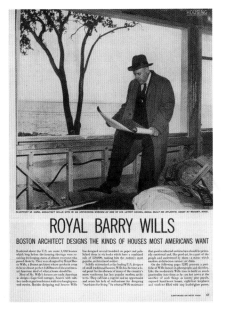

HAVING A WIFE IN CLUB OR CIVIC WORK THE APPROACH TO PRACTICE THE STALKING AND CAPTURE OF THE CLIENT

His prescriptions were catholic, involving everything from entering design competitions, mounting exhibitions, giving public lectures, serving on planning boards, and getting articles published, to "going to church more often than Easter and Christmas," as well as "Regulated social activity [is] not wasted in the charming company of your own competitors" and "Never [avoid] a friendly conversation with an apparently solvent person, even though he is a stranger."[10] Wills was somewhat reticent and a reluctant public speaker, so it is possible that his compendium was in part intended as self-prescribed medicine. If so, it was certainly effective.

Wills became a regular contributor to a wide variety of popular and professional journals, and made good use of reprints of every article they published. Before long his willingness to submit material and the increasing popularity of his work made him an attractive authority for magazine editors. In 1938 the editors of *Life* and *Architectural Forum*, both Henry Luce publications, produced a serialized feature they called "Eight Houses for Modern Living." The concept of architectural modernism, of forms ostensibly driven only by function, not tradition, had begun to circulate beyond the halls of design schools and art museums, and the two magazines came up with a novel way of presenting it to the public.

Seeking to exaggerate the differences between tradition and modernism-based concepts, the editors were able to convince four families, each representative of an income group of between $2,000 to $10,000 per year, and who wished to construct a new home, to choose their design by way of a competition. Each family was assigned two architects: one to design a traditional house, the other a modern design. Both were to suit the family's needs and budget, with an expectation that the family construct the house of their preference. The magazines would cleverly recoup their expense on the architects by offering the designs as mail-order cutout cardboard models and as full sets of blueprints, both of which proved exceptionally popular. Wills was one of the eight commissioned architects and was paired with a formidable figure, Frank Lloyd Wright, to design a home in the middle income $5,000 to $6,000 bracket.[11] Comfortable with the image, functionality, and respect for budget that the Wills design provided, it was his house that the Blackburn family selected and built.

Of course Wright was modern, but he did not represent the great tidal wave of professional and academic interest in modernism and its abstract functionalist aesthetic. Driven by profound dissatisfaction with the culture and traditions that had produced the unimaginable horror of World War I, modernism began in 1920s Europe as a deeply felt search for new values and a complete rejection of all artistic notions, including those that were architectural, that had come before. Spared the visceral confrontation with the war's carnage and destruction, America provided a less secure footing for its early stirrings. But that changed with the onset of the Great Depression and the coincidental emigration to the United States of a number of leading modern intellectuals, designers, and architects who fled the growing fascist presence in Europe, and who were embraced by many of the country's leading design schools.

Modernism was an intensely intellectual pursuit and found expression in a wide variety of architectural forms. But the International Style, a name coined to cover the range of designs on display at a famous exhibition at the Museum of Modern Art in New York in 1932, stuck as an all-encompassing moniker. To the untrained eye it quickly became shorthand for characteristically sleek, flat-roofed, rectangular, and monochromatic buildings. The International Style gained widespread favor in the United States for the design of commercial buildings, helped sell copious amounts of advertising copy in all manner of magazines, and completely transfixed the architectural academies and journals. But it never really caught on with the home- buying public, a fact not lost on the country's leading design and decorating magazines who invented any number of ways to raise this contradiction with their readership. In 1937 in an exhibition at Madison Square Garden sponsored by the *Ladies' Home Journal* and again in a 1938 promotion by *House & Garden* entitled "Your Home of Tomorrow," Wills was matched with such modernist luminaries as Le Corbusier and Richard Neutra, each time as a counterpoint to their visions of the future and a reminder of the importance and functionality of design that advocated some degree of continuity with the past.

It's not easy to describe the disjunction between the regard Wills was held in by many in the general public and those who longed for a modern world made with contemporary forms, but these two letters to the editor, appearing together in the September 16, 1946, issue of *Life* magazine give us a hint.

Sirs:

The American People on the whole are true to themselves and are proving it by surrounding themselves in the traditions of the great Americans who gave this country the firm foundation it has. It is no surprise to the student of the public that they are buying Royal Barry Wills architecture (Life, Aug 26) and buying good sound art to house in this architecture. It's time that the public be given credit for the good taste it is displaying all over the country. Charming houses, beautiful gardens, lovely furnishings, fine books, pictures and music are an accepted part of the American way of life.

Lillian B. Theme
Rockport, MA

If he was intimidated by the arguments or the company he was so often publicly paired with, Wills did not show it, providing as ever a humorous and insightful commentary on the issue at hand. His comment "Unfortunately Modern has come in too much as a style"[13] reveals how acute his eye was and how unswayed he was by the rhetoric surrounding a great deal of what was otherwise unremarkable contemporary design.

With an increasing portfolio of completed works and an expanding following in decorating and design journals, Wills hit upon the idea of publishing a book of his firm's houses. Featuring large pages filled with photographs and Wills's own very accomplished perspective drawings, *Houses for Good Living* (1940) and the subsequent *Better Houses for Budgeteers* (1941) were an unprecedented publishing success. Together with *This Business of Architecture* (1941) they had combined sales of over 520,000 copies by 1946, making him "the nation's most popular architectural author."[14]

His book publishing success coincided with the growth in house construction occurring as America, beginning to comprehensively mobilize industry to support the Allied cause in World War II, at last dug itself out of the Depression. It is said that when anticipation intensifies, the role of images also intensifies, and there was no question that America had developed a swelling backlog of housing demand, in mind and fact, during the previous decade. Suddenly, fully employed Americans had money to fulfill their dream of owning a home, and for many the vision of that home was a Colonial cottage. Reflecting back in the 1950s on the reasons for his success Wills freely admitted he had hit the "Cape Cod jackpot."[15]

But for architects, the economy that had found its legs supplying the Allies quickly evaporated with the priorities order of late 1941, which began restricting the use of vital materials and curtailed all nonmilitary activity. The impact was double edged, first because of the lack of conventional building projects, and secondly because the government agencies that controlled the essential war effort work generally considered architects too artistic and individualistic for building projects strained by the exigencies of war.[16]

"Thirty percent of all architects served in the Armed Forces, but only 39 percent of them, according to a survey by the AIA, performed some duty related to architecture. Of the remaining 70 percent left on the home front, only 29 percent found work in architecture."[17] Against such odds even the talented Wills struggled, though he was one of the fortunate few, most notably with the design and construction of the three-hundred-unit Lucy Mallory Defense Housing near Springfield, Massachusetts.

But while the war in the Pacific and Europe raged, another struggle was taking place on the home front. Disagreement about the causes and remedies for the Great Depression had been the centerpiece of economic and political debate in America well before the war. Now, even before the conflict was over, the argument about the most effective ways to avoid its return when the artificial stimulus from the war effort would go away became a titanic battle. Adding to the sense of urgency was the

looming need to house hundreds of thousands of returning service men and women, as well as the multitudes that had relocated to work in the wartime industries building ships, aircraft, and the materiel of war. Characteristically fought along party lines, the issue for the housing industry lay in the determination of the role government should play in the building process. Republicans, following the lead Herbert Hoover had provided over twenty years earlier, advocated strongly for involvement that would allow the private sector to turn the housing industry into a significant component of the economy, and thus the confinement of the government's role to the guaranteeing of loans for mortgages and large-scale land purchases. Democrats, on the other hand, were intent on ensuring that the significant portion of the population that would not be able to participate in home ownership would not be ignored. The debate, already emotional, became rancorous as the chief Republican

advocate, Senator Joe McCarthy, introduced claims that government-assisted and multifamily housing were "un-American" and "a breeding ground for Communists."[18] Under the circumstances, it is both remarkable that any legislation was passed and predictable that it was deeply flawed. But the legislation that culminated in the Housing Act of 1949 did succeed in completely transforming the domestic housing market.

Before the war, approximately one-third of all houses were built by their owners. Small contractors, who averaged fewer than five houses a year, built another third. By the late 1950s, aided by federal government programs such as the Federal Housing Administration (FHA) and government-backed lending for land purchases, about two-thirds of the new houses in the United States were produced by large builders. Backed by the Veterans Affairs (VA) and the FHA, the banks gave loans for ten million new homes between 1946 and 1953.[19] Vast speculative housing developments like Levittown in Long Island and Lakewood in California, each with more than fifteen thousand virtually identical homes, sprang up overnight, providing models for the industry that would forever change the American landscape. The housing market had expanded exponentially, but the role of the domestic architect was not keeping pace.

There is much evidence of the practicality Royal Barry Wills brought to his work. In his early publications, he listed, for instance, not the square footage of a house but rather its volume, in recognition of what the selected ceiling heights would have on the amount of material required, and thus the ultimate cost to be incurred. He also had success with selling complete designs through house plan services and Sunday editions of newspapers.[20] Now faced with the new realities of the post-war marketplace, Wills once again relied on logic to identify new opportunities to ply his trade.

The utmost in modern living is offered by this Luxury-Line Cape Cod home featured in February McCall's.

CAPE COD
BY ROYAL BARRY WILLS, F.A.I.A.

Fine Cape Cod styling is also available in Custom-Line homes, priced for the families of moderate income.

For those who prefer the traditional in home design, famed Royal Barry Wills, of Boston, Massachusetts, has created excitingly new National homes in Cape Cod styling. A characteristic simplicity gives these homes outstanding beauty and enduring charm.

Let your family experience the joy of living in a lovely Cape Cod National home. They are available in all sizes and price ranges.

1958 National homes also are designed in Colonial, Contemporary, and Southwest Modern styling by outstanding architects in these fields.

THE NATION'S LARGEST
PRODUCER OF QUALITY HOMES.

National HOMES

National Homes Corporation, Lafayette, Indiana

One avenue was the evolving prefabricated home manufacturing industry. In contrast to the newly minted large-scale subdivision and "community" builders, who were constructing hundreds of thousands of homes, almost all without the aid of an architect, prefabricated manufacturers relied heavily on design, and the brand of a well-known architect, to sell their products. Wills figured prominently in the growth of one of the nation's largest, National Homes Corporation. Incorporated in 1940 and initially focused on providing wartime housing, the business took off in 1948 with the creation of a modern assembly line offering an affordable two-bedroom house that could be erected in less than two weeks once a foundation had been poured. By 1956 more than 100,000 homes in an expanding range of offerings had been sold, increasing to more than 250,000 by 1963. Wills was featured prominently in the company's brochures and national advertising campaigns and worked closely with the manufacturing team to develop designs that met his strict visual criteria and the dictates of the prefabrication process.

As the 1950s drew to a close, Wills remained a fixture in the swirling discussions of the future of domestic architecture. In February 1960, *House & Home* magazine published "The New England Tradition and Royal Barry Wills, a New England Primer," with the following introduction:

> No one can say what part, if any, the New England tradition will play in the industrialized house of the later 1960s. But up to now New England prototypes have been some of America's most popular—and enduring—designs. This is especially true of the Cape Cod cottage—which has been one of the most seriously abused styles ever built.
>
> To show what the New England tradition really is, to see its essentials, *House & Home* presents here and on the following pages selections from the work of Royal Barry Wills. For 35 years Architect Wills has been building houses in the New England tradition. He is the acknowledged master of the style.[21]

Ever looking forward, Wills invested considerable time in creating a corporate structure for his firm that would facilitate its continuation as his own participation began to lessen. The value of his foresight became clear with his death in 1962, as the new ownership of Royal Barry Wills Associates carried on the firm's work without interruption, even as the housing market and industry have continued to evolve. House design that had once been applicable across the income spectrum has been increasingly pushed into the service of those who choose to avoid the dictates of mass production and have the means to do so. Yet in the more than fifty ensuing years, the firm's work has remained remarkably consistent, continuing to carefully balance the virtues and lessons of tradition with the exigencies and demands of contemporary life and commerce.

Royal Barry Wills designed not what he thought people should have, but rather what they so clearly wanted. He thought long and hard about the characteristics that would make that tradition-based image functional for contemporary American lifestyles and then applied his unerring eye and aesthetic judgment to make it beautiful and worthy of the heritage from which it was derived. He was tireless in the advocacy of his beliefs and unselfish in sharing his experience and lessons learned with his fellow architects who, in acknowledgement of his talent and service, elected him to a Fellowship in the American Institute of Architects in 1954.

And yet the annals of architectural history are largely silent on the Wills legacy. Chagrined over his persistent popularity for the construction of buildings so clearly based on a traditional past, and by the obvious if unwelcome confirmation of his belief in the wisdom of the American consumer, the architectural establishment largely ignored him. Fortunately, however, his legacy lies not in the silence architectural history books have afforded him, but rather in the extraordinary number and quality of the homes he gave to the nation—many with his own hand, and many more by those who had the benefit of being tutored under his discerning eye and able hand. For Wills, the most popular architectural author the country has ever seen, such a result would surely not be more welcome.

Houses

House in Narragansett

Narragansett has been a prominent seaside resort for over 150 years, and this house has been designed to recognize the depth and form of that tradition. But rather than being a historical recreation, it is a typical Wills house: a studied, artful composition of the elements from a way of building with a long tradition. Small panes of glass in multipaned windows, shingles for siding and roof that are left to weather to a soft grey, a prominent centered chimney, and simple trim at eaves and corners are all details that in character and form are used here to recall their Colonial forebears.

Here the design strategy of breaking down what might otherwise be an imposing house into a series of attached pieces, the numerous setbacks and changes in the roof pitch and height, the subtle asymmetrical alignment of doors and windows—all things that might have been found on a New England farmhouse that had grown out over time—reinforce the informality we expect and require in a setting for the convivial gathering of family and friends. This balancing act is reflected in the plan, too, which provides privacy for guests and owners and more formal areas for reflection and to host visitors, but which ultimately gives way to the contemporary, informal life that revolves around the kitchen and a communal gathering place, the great room.

The rambling plan shows the inherent flexibility of the traditional architectural theme and effectively combines modern-day necessities like a well-used access from the garage and mudroom, as well as the open kitchen/family room, with the privacy and separation of guest and family bedrooms and a more formal living and dining area. There is even a setback of one bay of the garage to ensure that it does not overpower the overall composition.

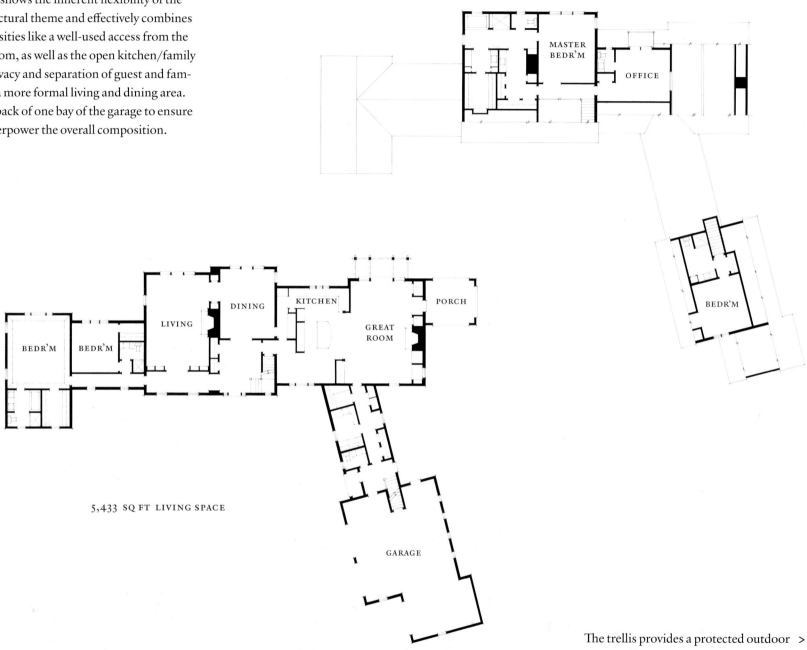

5,433 SQ FT LIVING SPACE

The trellis provides a protected outdoor > retreat adjacent to the living and dining rooms, and reduces the apparent scale of the tallest part of the rear of the house.

The number and variety of the ways that one can experience the outdoors, including the spectacular views from the second-floor bedrooms, adds greatly to the charm of living in or visiting the house.

The antique timber-framed barn was moved to and rebuilt on the site to provide space for a well-used communal recreation area. Its attractive patina portends well for what a few more seasons of weather will do for the adjacent house.

House in Maine

< Stone veneer and unstained wood siding empha-
size the rugged simplicity of this house. Curved
roofs are employed rarely by the firm, but this is
an occasion where the front entry porch benefits.

The prospect of a relaxed, unhurried life in the country is considerably enhanced in a setting of informal, domesticated rusticity.
Choosing the right materials is critical if one is to successfully
set such a stage. Here the palette of fieldstone and naturally weathering
clapboards and vertical boards perfectly complement the informal composition of the house and its attachments. The texture, detailing, and
finish of the materials, in conjunction with elements such as the antique
timber-framed entry porch, create a patina with a visceral appeal based,
as Royal himself had once observed, on their blend of age and honest
craftsmanship.

The size and shape of most of the elements that comprise the entry
façade have been chosen to at least raise the question of exactly how long
the house might have sat on this site. Even the first approach is carefully
choreographed, and potential distractions such as the doors of the large
garage are carefully shielded from view. The two fieldstone side walls
and their massive chimneys on the main body of the house emphasize
its centrality and importance but do so without overpowering the rustic,
domestic impression of this predominantly wooden structure.

The traditional rigor is relaxed on the less public, garden side of the
house, which contains considerably more glass than the entry side. Far
from schizophrenic, this change is instead the house's natural and en-
tirely appropriate response to the playful and unfettered life it is meant
to shelter and promote, rather like the loosening of a collar button
as one moves from the speeches to the small talk of an enjoyable and
memorable party.

A comfortable outdoor space at
the rear of the house.

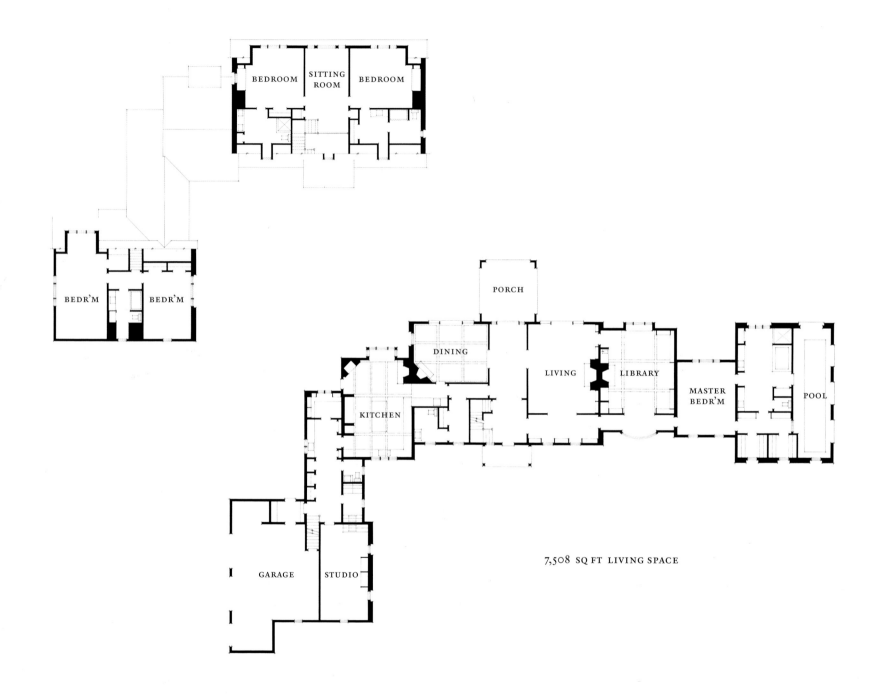

BEDROOM　SITTING ROOM　BEDROOM

BEDR'M　BEDR'M

PORCH

DINING

LIVING　LIBRARY

MASTER BEDR'M　POOL

KITCHEN

7,508 SQ FT LIVING SPACE

GARAGE　STUDIO

House in Maine

This small, informal two-bedroom house has a classic ground-hugging New England garrison profile, but its interior is open in ways that an ancestral colonialist bound to a fireplace as a single source of heat could have never imagined. The flat farmhouse red and dark window sash, inspired by the color of handmade paints from the eighteenth and nineteenth centuries, complement rather than contrast with the surrounding vegetation, effectively integrating the house into its wooded site. It may even suggest a memory of a New England landscape commonplace before so many of its forests were cleared to make way for agriculture. The consideration of the setting, a fundamental concern in the design of any traditionally inspired home, is therefore an important consideration in the choice of its color too.

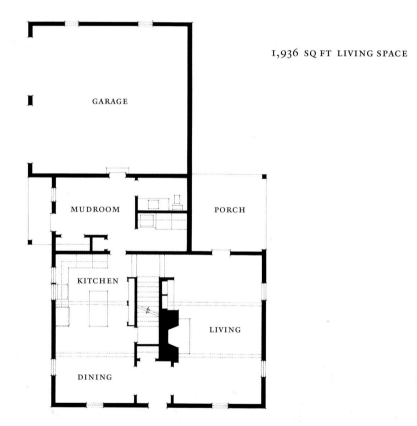

The charismatic garrison profile adds dis- >
tinction and character free of pretension to
a small house in the Maine woods.

1,936 SQ FT LIVING SPACE

The central fireplace and stair provide a hint of a colonial past, but the layout is unmistakably contemporary
and functional. A combined kitchen and dining room
open up the compact ground floor. This in turn is directly connected to the mudroom and garage, essential
components for coping with a life outdoors, pets and
implements, and the realities of harsh winters.

House in Islesboro

The four large chimneys and the overlapping gables of this house overlooking Penobscot Bay promise rooms of variety and purpose. But the only disappointment one would feel upon entering would come if one also harbored expectations of finding a warren of disconnected rooms and mismatched floor heights. For here the counterpoint to the carefully orchestrated and serendipitous exterior—the combination of whitewashed brick and clapboards, the barn-like garage, the manicured gravel courtyard one associates more with horses than with cars, the overflowing entry garden—is the exceedingly rational and elegant floor plan.

The deeply inset front door leads directly into the foyer, or stair hall, around which the life of the house is distributed. Privacy and formality for owners and guests to the right, children and guest quarters up the stairs, informal shared family life to the left. And throughout the enfilade of rooms, the conviviality one associates with a fireplace hearth is used to focus and give personality to the life of the major public rooms, including the family, dining, living, library, and enclosed porch. Enriched at the same time by the spectacular views to the water that almost every room enjoys, the house provides exactly the balance of eccentricity and order upon which a rich life might unfold.

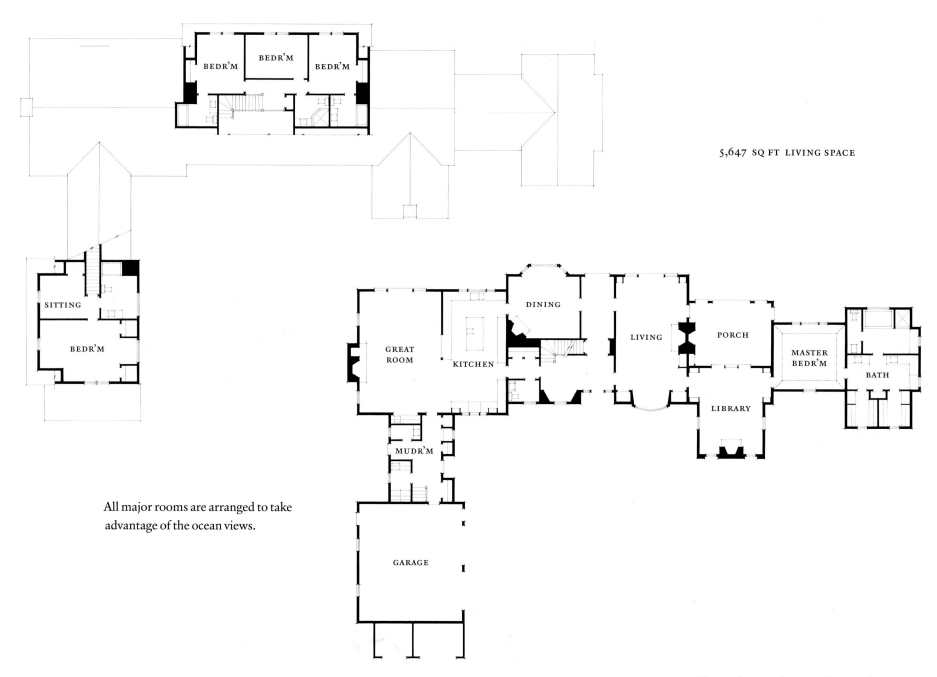

5,647 SQ FT LIVING SPACE

BEDR'M   BEDR'M   BEDR'M

SITTING

BEDR'M

GREAT ROOM

KITCHEN

DINING

LIVING

PORCH

MASTER BEDR'M

BATH

LIBRARY

MUDR'M

GARAGE

All major rooms are arranged to take advantage of the ocean views.

The sunken garden provides a welcoming >
transition to the front door.

An oval table with Windsor chairs fits >
comfortably in the bay-windowed dining
room that looks out over Penobscot Bay.

The kitchen opens up to an expansive
great room with a stone fireplace.

The fireplace on the screen porch is comfortable
on those cool summer evenings.

House in Maine

MID COAST, MAINE

Borrowing the irregular profile of a classic New England farmhouse that might have been built incrementally over generations is a popular Wills approach to adding a sense of history and permanence to a new home. But it has practical, not just aesthetic, applications, too. This house, built on a rocky knoll affording spectacular views, was designed to be built in two phases, and was indeed constructed that way. The plan's organizing principle is the orientation to the view, and is therefore drawn as an extended shallow arc that gives every room an equal share of the spectacle that unfolds below.

The house's low profile, emphasized by the gambrel roof used for the central block, seems to hug the earth, securing the building on its rocky perch. This strategy works to protect the view for those below as well, keeping the house in and not above the tree line.

The relationship to the site is further enhanced with the use of the locally quarried stone for the terraces, retaining walls and paving, and as a veneer for several prominent walls. As in all Wills houses, this veneer is eight to ten inches thick, carefully detailed at doors and windows to give the impression that it is the only material used to build the wall. Its integrity and choice as so prominent an element in the composition is wonderfully underscored by the natural rock outcropping that greets one along the walk to the deeply recessed front door.

< The exposed ledge indicates some of the challenges of building in the New England landscape. A singular tree and a stone-and-wood house anchored to the Maine bedrock.

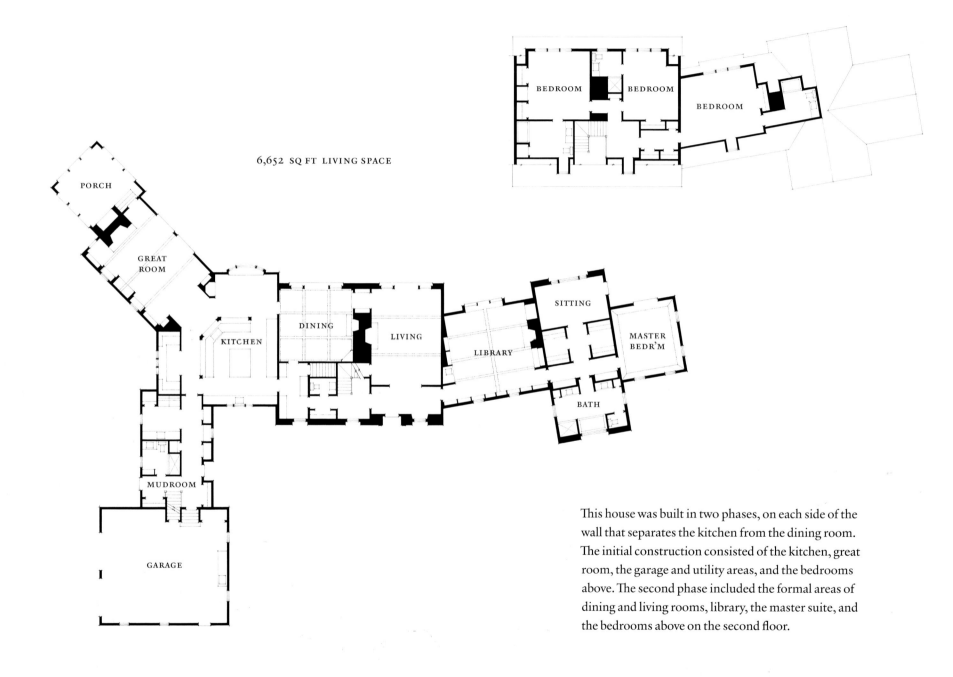

6,652 SQ FT LIVING SPACE

BEDROOM BEDROOM

BEDROOM

PORCH

GREAT
ROOM

KITCHEN

DINING

LIVING

SITTING

LIBRARY

MASTER
BEDR'M

BATH

MUDROOM

GARAGE

This house was built in two phases, on each side of the wall that separates the kitchen from the dining room. The initial construction consisted of the kitchen, great room, the garage and utility areas, and the bedrooms above. The second phase included the formal areas of dining and living rooms, library, the master suite, and the bedrooms above on the second floor.

A stone retaining wall and a finely wrought
balustrade mark the edge of the steeply sloping
site and define a linked series of view-oriented
outdoor living spaces.

House in Mamaroneck

MAMARONECK, NEW YORK

Although Royal Barry Wills had a wonderful ability to set the stage, he was not interested in simply putting up a scrim and asking his clients to suspend their disbelief. Wherever he could he attempted to give each house a sense of being utterly rooted to its particular location. This house, one of the last he designed, is a marvelous example of that preoccupation. Exterior materials that are venerable, like field stone, and that weather well, like wood shingles, are complemented with wide plank floors and salvaged hand-hewn ceiling beams to give a new house an immediate sense of unpretentious history. Royal was an unabashed antique hunter, and here the heavy timbers in the form of the "ships knees" that support the roof over the front entry are finds that were made after the original drawings of the house were completed, adding wonderfully to its personality and presence.

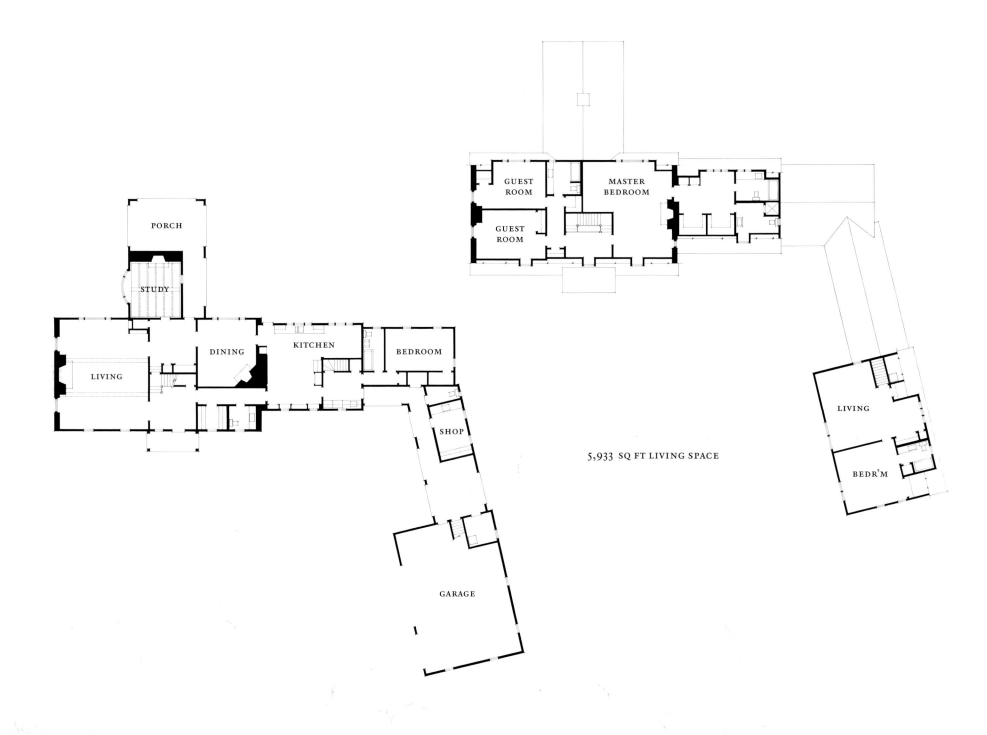

PORCH

STUDY

LIVING

DINING

KITCHEN

BEDROOM

SHOP

GARAGE

GUEST ROOM

GUEST ROOM

MASTER BEDROOM

LIVING

BEDR'M

5,933 SQ FT LIVING SPACE

The original drawings showed a much simpler post-and-bracket detail for the front entrance than what was ultimately built. Royal was able to locate the rare wood knee braces that constitute one of the most memorable visual elements on the house.

House in Oyster Harbors

The traditional detailing of this house—the fan-window-topped entrance, the twelve-over-twelve-paned windows, the twin chimneys that bracket the ends of the main façade, its interior molding and flooring—all confirm such an aspiration.

This house is large and formal enough so that the term *grand* would not be out of place, but any potential for unintended grandiloquence has been carefully tempered by the asymmetrical composition of the front façade, the playful arrangement of the ancillary wings, and by the use of less formal materials, such as the shingles used for siding. And if any confirmation of the intention in these acts is required, it is provided by a review of the interiors. Here it is obvious that the treasures it houses are meant to be used, not merely observed, a notion confirmed by the consistency with which they are employed throughout the rooms used for entertaining, relaxation, and work.

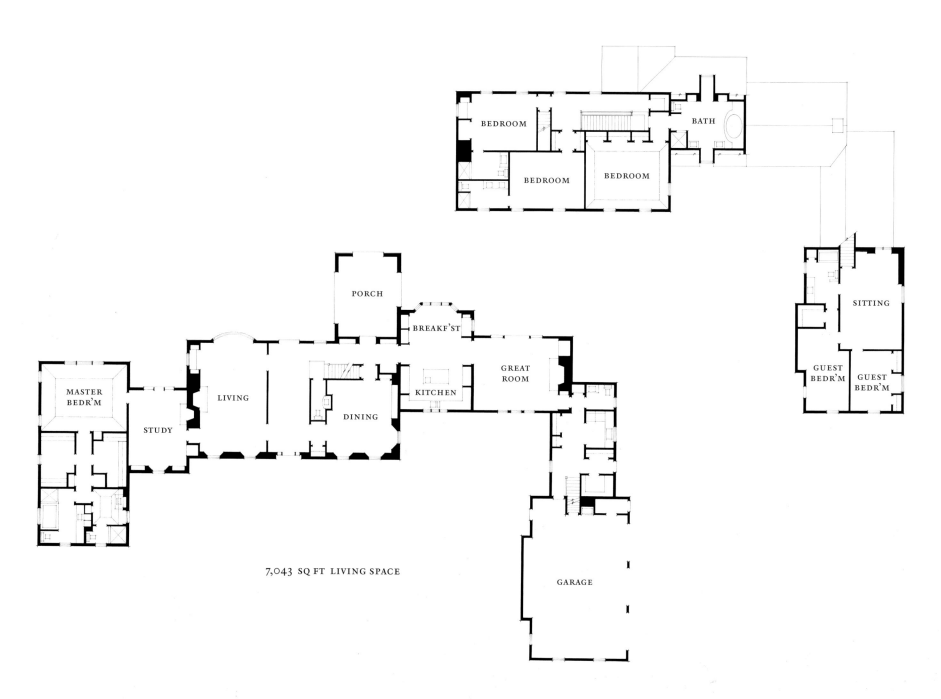

BEDROOM

BATH

BEDROOM   BEDROOM

SITTING

PORCH

BREAKF'ST

GREAT
ROOM

GUEST
BEDR'M   GUEST
                BEDR'M

MASTER
BEDR'M

LIVING

KITCHEN

STUDY   DINING

7,043 SQ FT LIVING SPACE

GARAGE

The front-to-back entrance foyer has a >
mural of local scenes. The wide-board
flooring has been hand stenciled.

House on Cape Cod

CAPE COD, MASSACHUSETTS

That a house is meant to be used and not merely observed is especially so when the setting is on Cape Cod and one must balance the rigors and pleasures of professional and recreational lives as lived by both family and guests. For this house on Cape Cod, what might otherwise become overt formality is softened with careful and understated detailing. Green shutters provide a contrast to the whitewashed brick, a finish chosen to provide an element of gracefully aging patina. The main body of the house, with its three dormers, paired front windows, and flanking large chimneys seems at first glance to be rigorously symmetrical. Only a second, slower look reveals the importance the single offset lantern to the left of the entry has in achieving this impression.

The house is asymmetrical front to back, too. As with a number of RBW Associates houses, the front is more traditional, the windows smaller, and the detailing what one would expect of a traditional house. Only in the rear is the more casual, domestic aspect of the house revealed, in the larger and more frequent windows and the multiple doors that allow the house to open to the outdoors. In this it is easy to appreciate why a Wills house is often referred to as a good neighbor.

7,822 SQ FT LIVING SPACE

BEDR'M   SITTING   BEDR'M

SITTING

BEDR'M   BEDR'M

MASTER
BEDR'M

LIVING

DINING

LIBRARY

KITCHEN   SITTING   PORCH

GARAGE

Guest House Floor Plan

SITTING

KITCHEN

LIVING

BEDR'M   BEDR'M

1,485 SQ FT LIVING SPACE

Guests can enjoy their privacy in
this two-bedroom cottage.

House in Chatham

CHATHAM, MASSACHUSETTS

The "half Cape" is one of the most versatile styles in traditional residential architecture and can be, and has been, adapted to almost any scale and practically any site. Historically, smaller proportions are the rule, and this three-bedroom house certainly alludes to the past with its precise, almost diminutive compositional rigor. A large central chimney, narrow clapboards graduated near the grade, naturally weathered shingles, and fenced-in dooryard garden all help create a composition of domestic simplicity. Full-length shutters help to frame the doors and emphasize the human scale of the entrances, which are themselves differentiated by the small panes inserted above the main entry. Of particular note is the V-style gutter with custom-designed brackets, a detail that gives visual weight to the edge of the roof on the main body of the house.

In a break from tradition, the house is oriented away from the road, which gives it a reserved and sheltered feel. In this case, the garage, often a visual liability, is designed instead as a barn. Its loft door, hay davit, and cupola, in combination with gracefully arched doors, together present an attractive alternative façade to the street.

The plan is informal and compact, but great care has been applied to creating effective transitional spaces between public and private areas of the house. Built-in bookcases help frame the opening between the breakfast room and great room without closing either area off.

BEDROOM

BEDROOM

BAR

GREAT ROOM

DINING

KITCHEN

BEDROOM

GARAGE

2,571 SQ FT LIVING SPACE

House in Maine

The gambrel-style roof is the practical answer to achieving more space on the second floor than that afforded by the traditional Cape. Here the roof pitches on the main body of the house have been carefully chosen to ensure that the visual result is not too top heavy. And to the rear, a large flat shed dormer further expands the utility of the second floor with additional headroom and light for otherwise-impossible-to-accommodate bathrooms.

This deeply practical approach is reflected in the importance the mudroom and ancillary service areas have in the plan and the way the house is used. The front elevation of the main body of this small house is rigorously symmetrical and thus formal: an effect enhanced by the central chimney, dormers, and paired windows, and to which is given added substance by the heavy V-style gutter. The lack of a sidewalk leading to, what to the world is, the front door confirms that the role of this elevation is largely symbolic, but does nothing to diminish the veracity of the entire composition.

BEDR'M

BEDROOM

BEDROOM

2,878 SQ FT LIVING SPACE

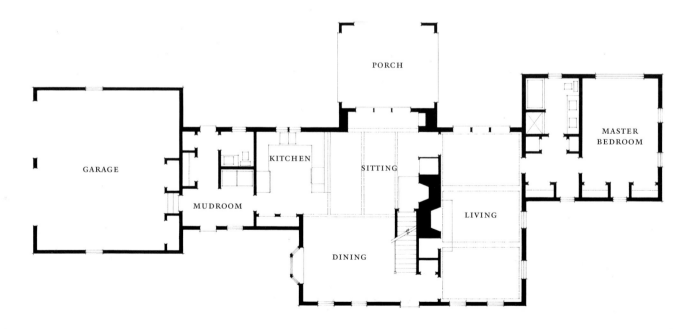

PORCH

GARAGE

KITCHEN

SITTING

MASTER
BEDROOM

MUDROOM

LIVING

DINING

House in West Harwich

WEST HARWICH, MASSACHUSETTS

In 1932, in the midst of the Great Depression, Royal Barry Wills submitted a design for a small house to a national competition sponsored by *Better Homes and Gardens* magazine that was sanctioned by then President Herbert Hoover. Wills's modest three-bedroom Cape ended up winning a Presidential Gold Medal and provided valuable publicity during a most challenging economic period. The house he created, which was eventually built for William Itmann, deliberately avoided the stripped-down modern aesthetic that was quickly gaining favor among the contemporary architectural elite. Instead, he showed how adaptable to modern requirements a Cape Cod–inspired house could be, including critical amenities like bathrooms on both floors and closets for all the bedrooms, while adapting its geometry to the confines of a suburban building lot.

Seventy-five years later the design of the Gold Medal house came full circle when the firm was approached by the Vargus family on Cape Cod who wanted a year-round house that would suit their lifestyle. Their needs were straightforward—casual first-floor gathering spaces and three second-floor bedrooms for them and their two children—and they had seen the Gold Medal House in the 1940 Royal Barry Wills book,

Houses for Good Living. The plan of that house, slightly expanded, would fit their living style and also their own small Cape Cod lot, with enough room for a four-season room and a garage.

A comparison of the two houses is instructive for several reasons. It clearly shows, for instance, how modern expectations and lifestyles have evolved, and how adaptable the Cape is to those evolving living arrangements. But perhaps most importantly it shows how modern was the approach Wills had adopted in the first third of the last century.

Both houses include garages, though the original house took advantage of a sloping site that allowed it to be tucked under the first floor. In the new house, the garage is attached to the house with a four-season sitting room adjacent to a full bathroom and a laundry room. The new arrangement elaborates on the vital element of a modern mudroom entrance and includes a wood stove that was specifically requested by the family.

A small study adjacent to a front stair hall are features of both houses and provide a subtle contrast to the more casual and open spaces in the plan. The study can also function as a guest bedroom, thanks to its proximity to the downstairs bathroom. Carefully detailed built-in cabinetry, a hallmark of Royal Barry Wills, is strategically employed in both houses.

The biggest difference in the house floor plans lies in the relationship between the kitchen and the other areas of the house. Food preparation wasn't the social activity that it is today, and older appliances and ventilation systems didn't perform as efficiently as modern ones. The Vargus kitchen is larger and directly connected with the dining room in a way that doesn't interfere with circulation in the kitchen work areas. It is also served by a generous pantry located near the hall that leads to the side entry and garage.

Another important difference is in the overall scale and proportions of the new dwelling. Ceiling heights have been raised and the overall sizes of rooms and hallways have been expanded slightly.

The open dining and kitchen space of the Vargus house leads directly into a living room in exactly the same way as the 1932 house. The relationship between the fireplace and a modern entertainment system poses a challenge that did not exist seven decades ago, but the proportions of the room allow for two seating arrangements. The slightly off-center location of the fireplace is balanced by a window seat that completes the informal quality of the space.

The proportions of the new house also make for more generous bedrooms upstairs. While the room layout is nearly identical, a dormer window has been omitted in the new house to improve the layout of a second-floor bedroom. A curious feature of both houses is a false central chimney, whose placement was mandated by the need for visual harmony on the exterior. The one in the Vargus house conceals a small skylight that brightens the upper stair hall.

The exterior treatment of both the new and the old house is similar in its unpretentious use of painted wood clapboards on the primary façade and cedar shingles on the gable ends. The Vargus house employs flush boards on the garage for contrast, but its period reproduction light fixtures match the ones used on the 1932 house nearly exactly. As a final detail in homage to the original, a simple white picket fence defines an entry courtyard with a traditional bluestone walkway.

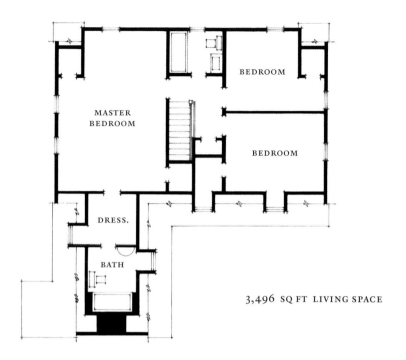

BEDROOM

MASTER
BEDROOM

BEDROOM

DRESS.

BATH

3,496 SQ FT LIVING SPACE

DINING

PANTRY

KITCHEN

STUDY

LIVING

ITMANN HOUSE: This house was built in 1932 in Brookline, Massachusetts. The photo and plan have been flipped to aid comparison with the new house.

VARGUS HOUSE: This house is a fresh interpretation of a design that earned Royal Barry Wills a Presidential Gold Medal in 1932 for the best small house in America.

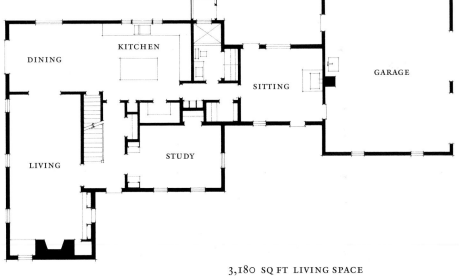

3,180 SQ FT LIVING SPACE

House in Maine

T he recognition of the importance of phasing—of where it is logical to add on and how to build in increments that seem complete in and of themselves—characterizes many RBW Associates houses.

This house on the rocky coast of Maine exemplifies the value of this approach. Its composition, derived from the fanciful notion of Colonial-era incremental expansion, and exaggerated by the changes in material and the way the eaves of the main house and the mudroom/service wing are intentionally misaligned, lends itself perfectly to a future addition. The logic is enhanced by organizing the plan to ensure that the future master bedroom wing does not compromise circulation or the light and views enjoyed by the first-phase rooms.

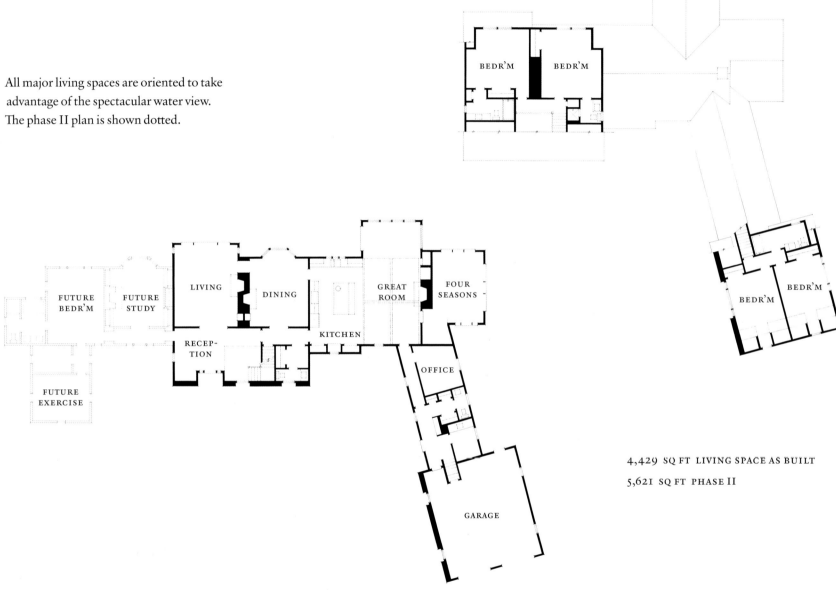

All major living spaces are oriented to take
advantage of the spectacular water view.
The phase II plan is shown dotted.

BEDR'M BEDR'M

FUTURE
BEDR'M

FUTURE
STUDY

LIVING

DINING

GREAT
ROOM

FOUR
SEASONS

RECEP-
TION

KITCHEN

FUTURE
EXERCISE

OFFICE

BEDR'M

BEDR'M

GARAGE

4,429 SQ FT LIVING SPACE AS BUILT

5,621 SQ FT PHASE II

All major rooms are oriented toward the spectacular water view.

Master bedroom with its view of
Vineyard Sound.

House on Martha's Vineyard

CHILMARK, MASSACHUSETTS

The spectacular views of Vineyard Sound and Gay Head that this house enjoys have previously inspired the design of a number of houses that, in their height and mass, raised the ire of the local community. As a result, the design of this house is constrained not just by a steeply sloping site perpendicular to the view, but by a severe height restriction.

The house, by mandate largely a single story, is stretched out across the slope, oriented so that every room benefits from the ocean views. But to avoid becoming a long uninterrupted bar, it is divided into a series of pavilions—marked with balconies, porches, dormers, octagonal roofs, and gables—that each present different ways of experiencing the view.

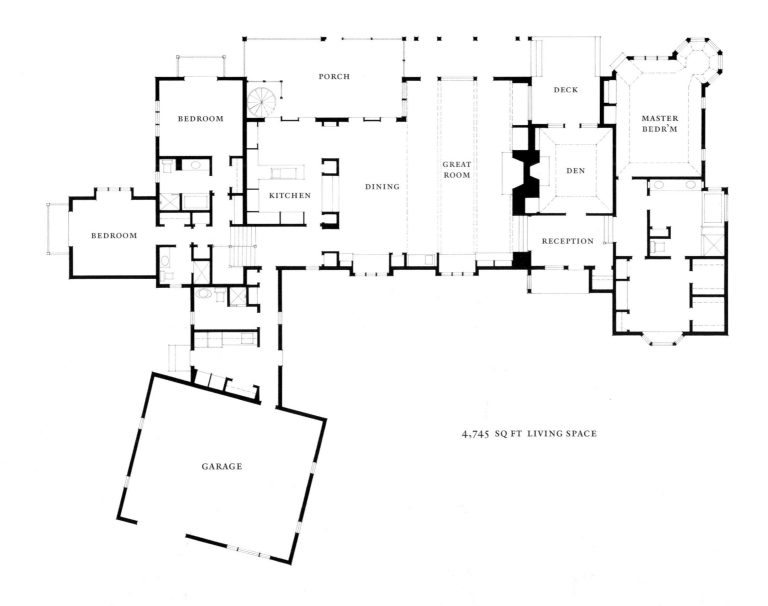

BEDROOM

BEDROOM

PORCH

KITCHEN

DINING

GREAT
ROOM

DECK

DEN

RECEPTION

MASTER
BEDR'M

4,745 SQ FT LIVING SPACE

GARAGE

House in New London

There are many considerations taken into account in the design of a new house. Some are related to its size and function, some to budget and schedule, and of course, some to what it might look like. But the element that binds the house to the life the owners wish for it, and which will determine the depth of the satisfaction it affords, is how its design responds to its particular location. Is the site rolling or flat, wooded or open? What are the views and from where are they available? What is the nature of the light and what is its path over the course of a day and the seasons? What is the route one takes in first seeing the house and then to arrive at the front door? What are the local building traditions and materials?

Done well, the result of such design consideration is a house that not only accommodates functional requirements, but pays its hosts the perpetual compliment of seeming, as it does here, of always having been there. The house's fit on this hill overlooking Lake Sunapee is further enhanced by the firm's time-tested method of paying homage to the way the original farm buildings in this part of the world evolved over time. The soundness of this notion, which might be described as form following fiction—the implication that the house was built in stages when, in fact, it was built all at once, or that it was once home to livestock, tool and machinery storage, and rooms for separating milk or making cheese, instead of just to people—is proven here not just by the house's satisfying appearance or the superb practicality of its plan, but also by the ease with which it accommodates the requirements of a real barn.

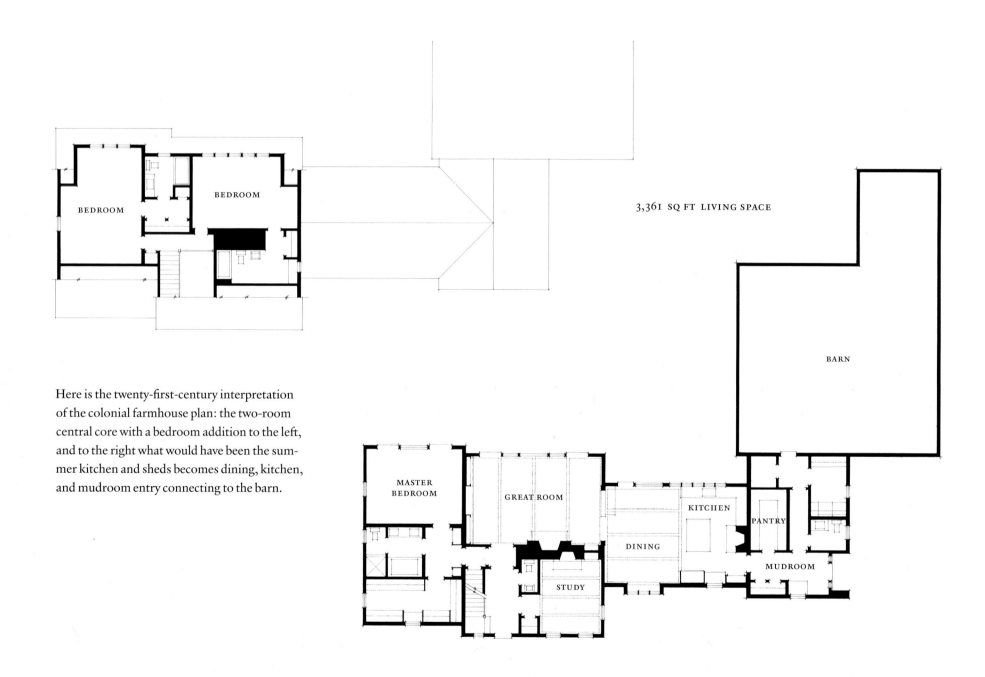

BEDROOM

BEDROOM

3,361 SQ FT LIVING SPACE

BARN

Here is the twenty-first-century interpretation of the colonial farmhouse plan: the two-room central core with a bedroom addition to the left, and to the right what would have been the summer kitchen and sheds becomes dining, kitchen, and mudroom entry connecting to the barn.

MASTER BEDROOM

GREAT ROOM

KITCHEN

DINING

PANTRY

STUDY

MUDROOM

The bluestone terrace and pool provide
relaxing spots from which to enjoy
the spectacular view.

House on Cape Cod

Combining formality with a sense of the urbane is a most appropriate approach to the design of larger homes. It is especially suited to this house on Cape Cod, which began with a requirement for an elegant and expansive ground floor suitable for grand-scale entertaining. The large, symmetrical two-story mass of the central block commands the entry courtyard, which it presents with a suitable and unmistakable formal entry. But great care has been given to imbue the overall composition with qualities that celebrate the human qualities of the design. The dormers and shutters, the asymmetrical flanking wings (one for the kitchen, the other for bedrooms), the use of the whitewashed brick, even the specially designed chimney caps (required to discourage nesting osprey from commandeering them), all give the house not only presence but personality.

The rear of the house literally opens out to the water on which it is set, and the sloping site is carefully laid out to accommodate amenities such as a pool and a putting green without allowing them to detract from the composed views from the rooms or their adjoining porches and verandas.

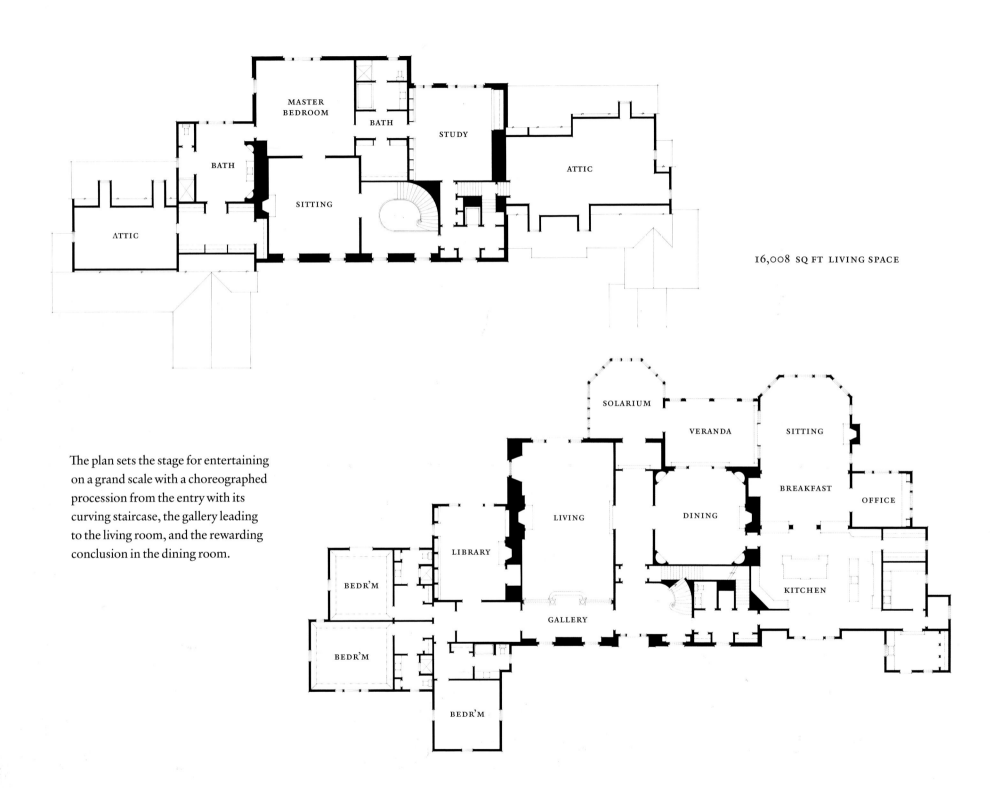

MASTER BEDROOM

BATH

STUDY

BATH

ATTIC

SITTING

ATTIC

16,008 SQ FT LIVING SPACE

The plan sets the stage for entertaining on a grand scale with a choreographed procession from the entry with its curving staircase, the gallery leading to the living room, and the rewarding conclusion in the dining room.

SOLARIUM

VERANDA

SITTING

BREAKFAST

OFFICE

LIVING

DINING

LIBRARY

KITCHEN

BEDR'M

BEDR'M

GALLERY

BEDR'M

The courtyards are contained by smaller-scaled, shingle-clad wings.

House in Wenham

WENHAM, MASSACHUSETTS

While the provincial styles of French origin are not ones normally associated with the Colonial Revival, they certainly have a long tradition of use in many parts of New England. Evocative and romantic, they have endured in part because of their ability to stir the emotions, a highly desirable characteristic in the adventure that comes with building the house of one's dreams.

In this house in Wenham, Massachusetts, the playful organization around the entry court, enlivened with its variety of dormers, bays, and varying roof planes, adds to the drama and keeps what is, in fact, a large house from becoming too formal or imposing. Together with the landscape, which includes carefully preserved mature trees and traditional crushed stone for the drive, these devices begin to suggest images that heighten one's anticipation of what lies within.

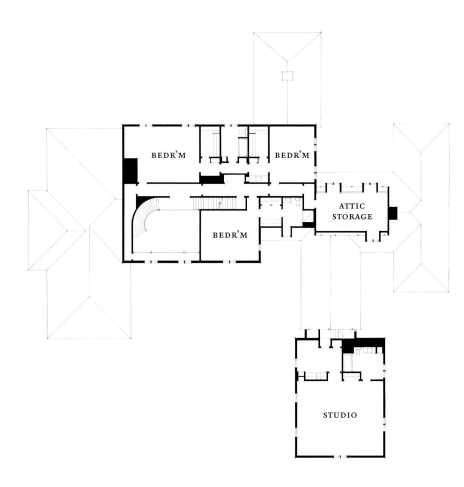

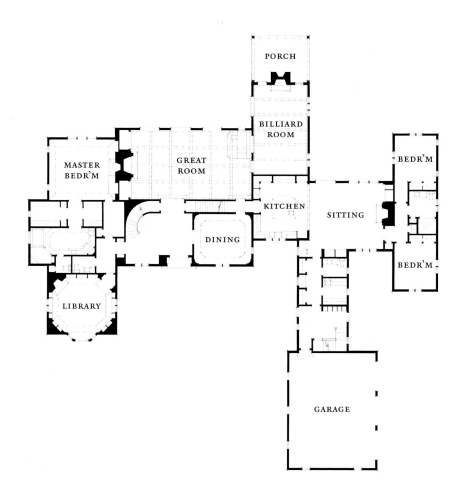

9,822 SQ FT LIVING SPACE

The plan fulfills the promise offered by the exterior design, providing a highly individualized layout suited to the owner's interests and lifestyle.

A stand of massive oak trees at the rear
of the house was preserved during the
construction process.

House in Weston

WESTON, MASSACHUSETTS

Brick is an extraordinarily versatile material, but one that, especially when painted, can appear monolithic. On this house in Weston, Massachusetts, this potential liability is turned into a wonderful foil for an exposition on the importance carefully considered details play in the creation of successful design. Here, seemingly small elements: the exaggerated corners of the main block, using a pattern known as quoining; the irregular shape and texture of the brick that was chosen; the dormers that break the eave line; the exactness and alignment of the downspouts; the shutters flanking the ground floor windows and the entry door, all take a simple volume and turn it into something that attracts and holds the eye.

These details are complemented by the composition of the pieces— the two massive but asymmetrically placed chimneys, the flanking clapboard-clad outdoor porch and bedroom extension, the more casual organization of the façade facing the backyard—which provide further visual richness and counterpoint to the rigorously geometrical outline of the main brick body of the house.

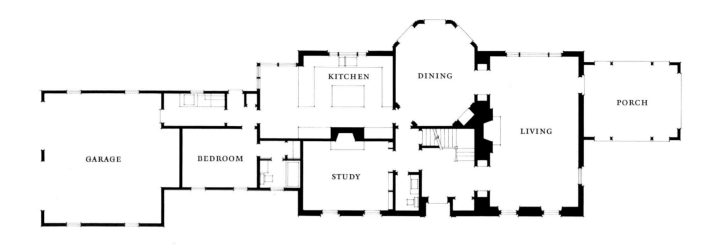

KITCHEN   DINING

PORCH

GARAGE   BEDROOM   LIVING

STUDY

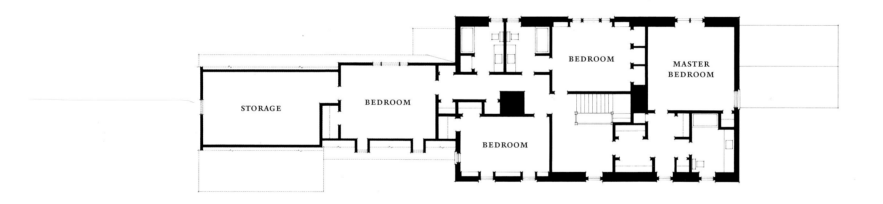

STORAGE   BEDROOM   BEDROOM   MASTER BEDROOM

BEDROOM

If it is difficult to judge the age of the house from
the outside, as it is with almost any RBW Associates
house, an examination of the floor plan, particularly
of the size of bedrooms and bathrooms, can provide
useful forensic evidence.

4,912 SQ FT LIVING SPACE

House in Walpole

WALPOLE, MAINE

As those who have experienced it will know, a forest is far from a static thing, and living in the woods is very different from living in a wooded setting. In Maine, two of the design issues posed are how to balance a sense of privacy with one of security, and a sense of arrival with the practical demands of clearing snow in the winter. Here the predominant response is not in how the house is laid out—experience has shown that within certain limits people's requirements are not so dissimilar—but how it is oriented to the site. The garage is the first element one encounters—when clearing snow every extra foot counts—but it is via an oblique view that is further softened with the elliptical openings used for the garage doors. The essential mudroom is the everyday working access and is inset under the cover of a recessed porch. But a clear path outlined by a tended small perennial garden leads one securely to the formal front entry should circumstances or decorum demand.

The massive chimney is a crucial element in the overall design. For, in addition to providing a strong profile against the sky, it anchors the main living areas of the house, providing fireplaces in the great room and the library and serving as the armature around which the stair winds to the second floor.

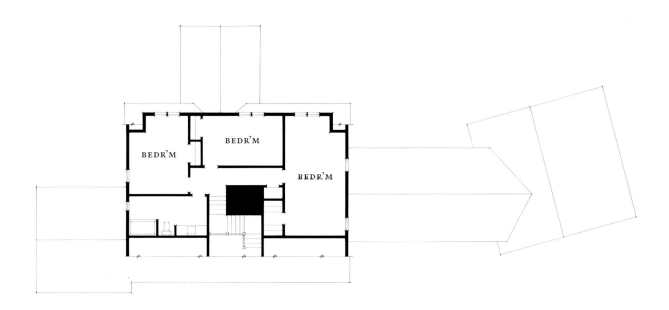

3,160 SQ FT LIVING SPACE

A typical full Cape with center entrance, two windows on each side, and a central chimney; but an atypical plan with the kitchen in the ell and a first-floor master bedroom.

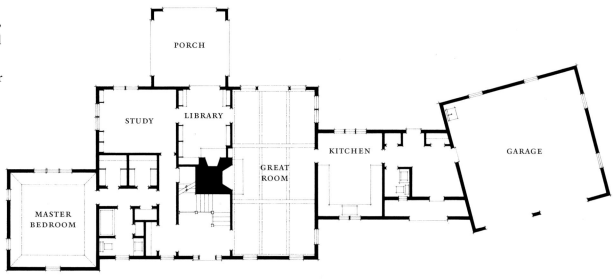

House in Weston

The whitewashed brick, long windows and shutters, hip roof appendage, and curved-roof dormers add what its designers playfully describe as a "French twist" to this informal but elegant home in Weston, Massachusetts. Nestled among mature hardwoods and behind a gently curving stone terrace wall that defines the entry drive court, the house exudes the sort of charm one might associate with a very civilized life removed to the country.

The house hugs the ground, a quality that helps it seem smaller and much less imposing than its large size and number of rooms might otherwise suggest. This impression of being a sophisticated cottage rather than a small manor house is further enhanced by the carefully studied proportions of the dormers and chimneys, and by the scale and character of the surrounding gardens.

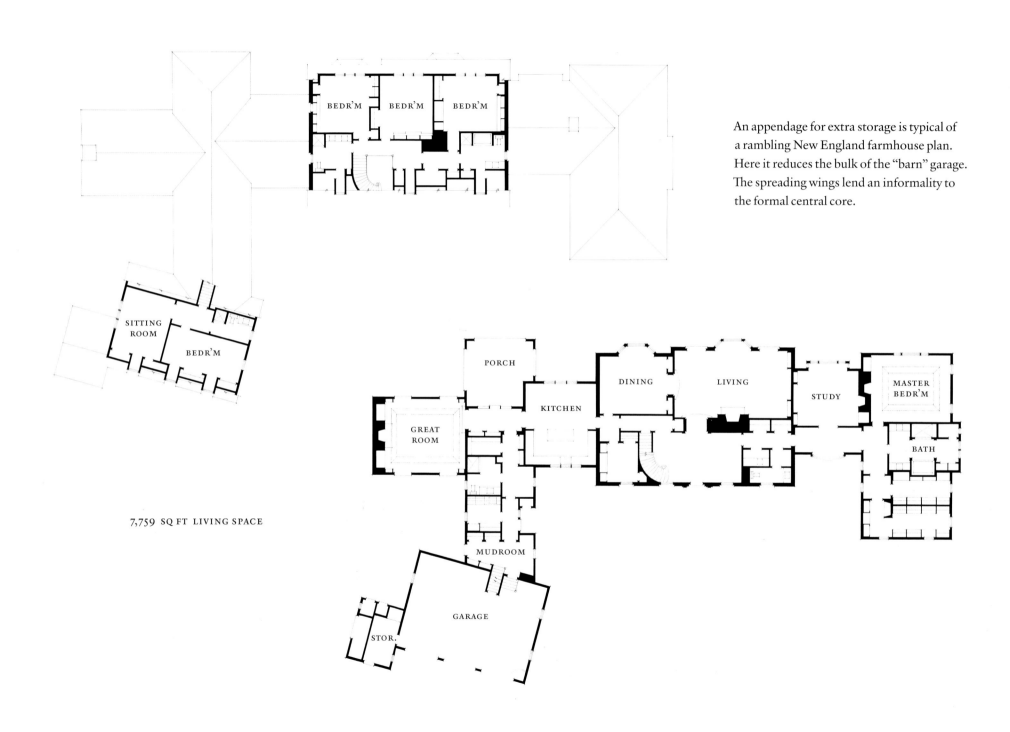

An appendage for extra storage is typical of a rambling New England farmhouse plan. Here it reduces the bulk of the "barn" garage. The spreading wings lend an informality to the formal central core.

BEDR'M BEDR'M BEDR'M

SITTING ROOM

BEDR'M

7,759 SQ FT LIVING SPACE

PORCH

KITCHEN

DINING LIVING

STUDY

MASTER BEDR'M

GREAT ROOM

BATH

MUDROOM

GARAGE

STOR.

House on Cape Cod

CAPE COD, MASSACHUSETTS

This house on Cape Cod is a seemingly straightforward execution of a classic Wills approach. It features a gracious front entry embraced by the extended wing of the garage, its doors turned away from the entry and connected to the house with a mudroom, and a series of ancillary wings for bedrooms and kitchen flanking a main volume containing the principal living areas. The irregular shape, mortar stains, and articulated coursing pattern of the reclaimed brick that is the principal façade material provide a pleasing patina that also hints at the informal retreat the house offers.

That promise is fulfilled by the floor plan, which is a departure from the norm. Here the entire second floor is given over to the owners' master suite, a sanctuary that leaves the ground floor free for the use of family and frequent guests.

MASTER BEDR'M

BATH

6,655 SQ FT LIVING SPACE

BEDR'M

BEDR'M

DINING

LIVING

BEDR'M

SITTING

LIBRARY

KITCHEN

BEDR'M

GARAGE

House in Hopkinton

HOPKINTON, NEW HAMPSHIRE

Some houses exude formality; others grudgingly accept the need for its existence. In doing so, they sometimes give reason for one to confuse informality with a lack of concern for intention. This house in Hopkinton, New Hampshire, presents no such contradictions. For although a review of the plan clearly shows the emphasis given to the informal, everyday working and living areas of the house—the kitchen, sitting and great rooms—the extraordinary care given to the composition of house, barn, pool house, and complementary landscape make it clear that here appearances are a matter of considered choice, not circumstance.

Whereas in some Wills Associates houses the use of stone veneer is used to create a contrast in an otherwise straightforward picture, here the commonality in garden wall and building façade lock the house to the site and to a regional tradition of building with the local bounty of timber and stone.

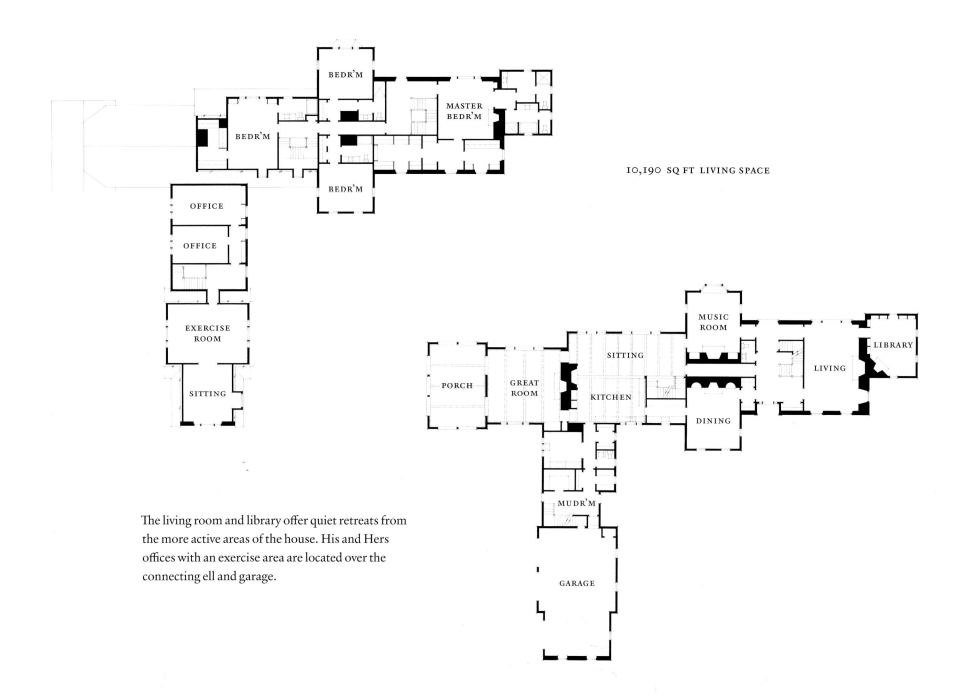

BEDR'M

MASTER BEDR'M

BEDR'M

BEDR'M

10,190 SQ FT LIVING SPACE

OFFICE

OFFICE

EXERCISE ROOM

SITTING

MUSIC ROOM

SITTING

LIBRARY

PORCH

GREAT ROOM

KITCHEN

LIVING

DINING

MUDR'M

GARAGE

The living room and library offer quiet retreats from the more active areas of the house. His and Hers offices with an exercise area are located over the connecting ell and garage.

The barn involved collaboration with a local timber frame company. The restrained form and detailing help reduce its scale.

An arched side entry provides
a moment of reduced scale.

House in Weston

T his house in Weston, Massachusetts, is ingeniously designed to maximize the utilization of a choice but confined lot surrounded by conservation land and a golf course. The design turns the skewed geometry of the site boundaries into a virtue that aligns the long extending arm of the kitchen/great room/mudroom/garage against a lot line, beautifully enclosing the private and serene entry courtyard. The design's ability to satisfy the owners' specific request for a house suitable for entertaining is amplified by the strategy of visually "borrowing" the surrounding open and impressive landscape.

The constrained lot required that a number of amenities, including a media room, pool, and gym, be provided in a further level beneath the main floor (not shown in plan). Far from being confined to a basement, their significance in the life of the house is revealed by the curving stair that has been provided to them from the entry hall.

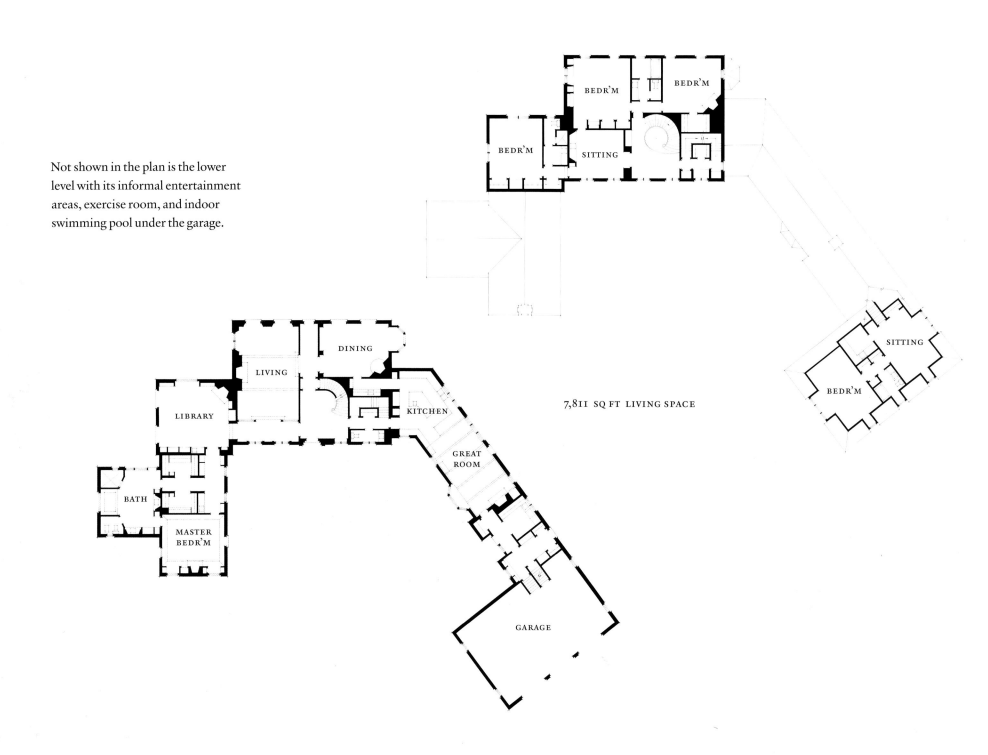

Not shown in the plan is the lower level with its informal entertainment areas, exercise room, and indoor swimming pool under the garage.

BEDR'M

BEDR'M

BEDR'M

SITTING

SITTING

BEDR'M

7,811 SQ FT LIVING SPACE

DINING

LIVING

LIBRARY

KITCHEN

GREAT ROOM

BATH

MASTER BEDR'M

GARAGE

House in Osterville

While for many, a Cape Cod vacation is a two-week excursion, this house is home to a family that has chosen to divide their time between town and shore, and it is used as a year-round residence. Its design is therefore a function of balancing the implied informality of a country retreat with the needs, both functional and aesthetic, of full-time use.

The composition made with a series of varying rooflines, gables, and projections is given refinement and repose by the consistent use of wood shingle siding and the conservatively detailed white trim around windows and doors. The wonderful light-filled interior is the result of the orientation to the spectacular water view, which also gives the house its varying front and waterside personalities. The distinctive gambrel roof on the rear is here used as a device to provide the space necessary to ensure that the three major upstairs bedrooms are equivalent in size as well as their embrace of the water view, while avoiding the monotony that would result from simply stringing out three identical spaces.

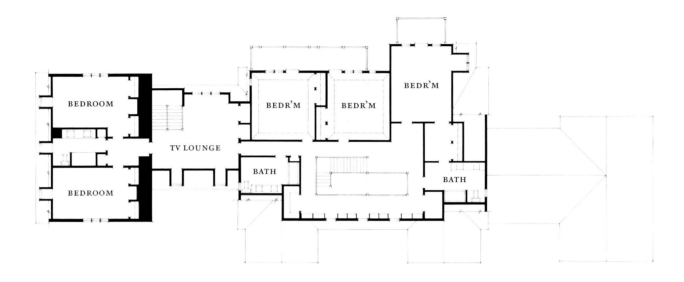

BEDROOM

BEDROOM

TV LOUNGE

BEDR'M

BEDR'M

BEDR'M

BATH

BATH

The formal character of the reception hall and the flanking dining room and library gives way to the graduated assembly of living spaces that enjoy expansive water views.

7,079 SQ FT LIVING SPACE

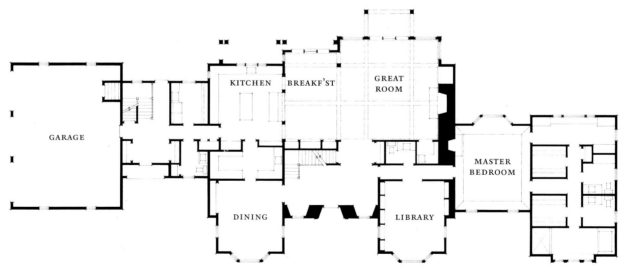

GARAGE

KITCHEN

BREAKF'ST

GREAT ROOM

DINING

LIBRARY

MASTER BEDROOM

House in Prides Crossing

T his house in Prides Crossing, Massachusetts, was built on a site that included an existing barn. The program for the new home— the list of desired functional spaces and their sizes—suggested a house of impressive proportions. Detailed with shutter-flanked traditional twelve-over-twelve windows, and organized around a classic center hall entry, the otherwise straightforward design is given a degree of informality by the size, variety, and orientation of the ancillary wings and through the use of the stone veneer. The impression is enhanced considerably through the use of the same material for the stone wall that defines the entry courtyard.

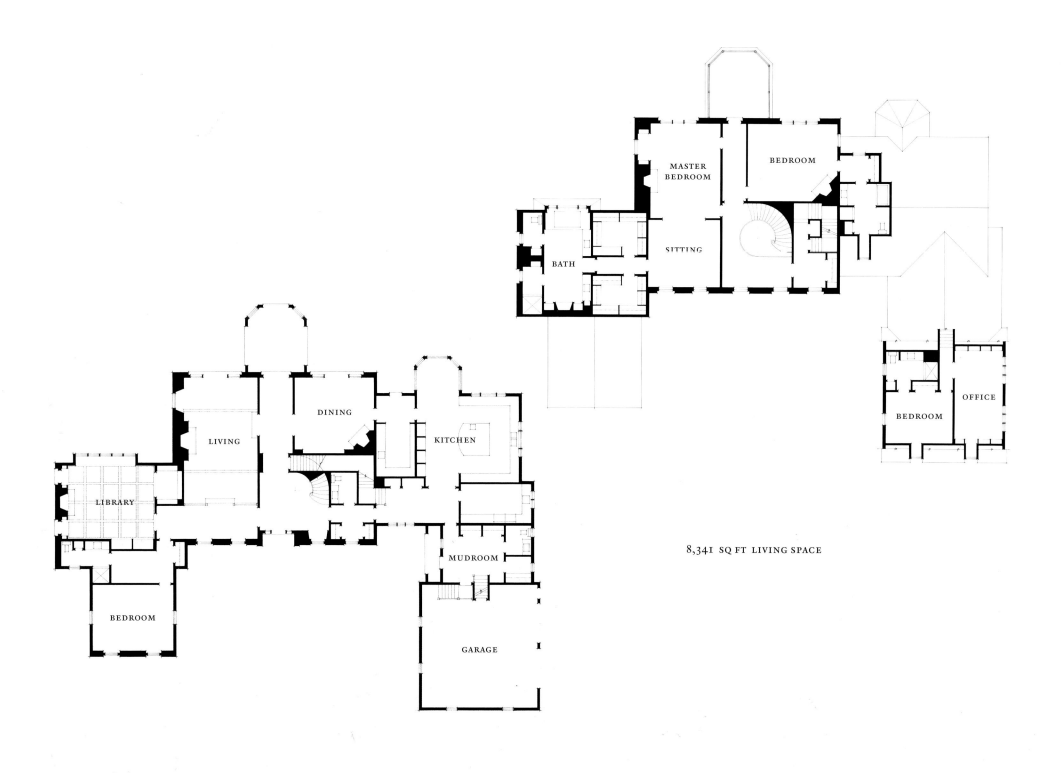

MASTER
BEDROOM

BEDROOM

BATH

SITTING

BEDROOM

OFFICE

DINING

KITCHEN

LIVING

LIBRARY

MUDROOM

BEDROOM

GARAGE

8,341 SQ FT LIVING SPACE

TOP: The two-story window is at the end of the entrance hall behind the circular stair.
BOTTOM: The casual family room as furnished when the house was first constructed.

House in Weston

WESTON, MASSACHUSETTS

Every design requires a starting point, and in this case it was provided by the client's request for a grand glass-feature window. The spectacular two-story stair hall that greets the eye upon entry from the front door leaves an indelible impression that easily satisfies that requirement while simply organizing the separation of the formal and private wing of the house from the everyday and more casual areas.

The use of whitewashed brick lends sophistication to the typical clapboard, shingles, and flush boarding of Colonial Revival houses, and this house is no exception. Here the desire to create a visual impression of a house built of combined increments is accentuated by the use of variably spaced roof dormers. The two photographs of the front of the house also illustrate its changes over time. In the version that features the large tree in the center of the driveway turnaround, one can just see the increased height of the expanded master bedroom suite the firm added for a subsequent owner.

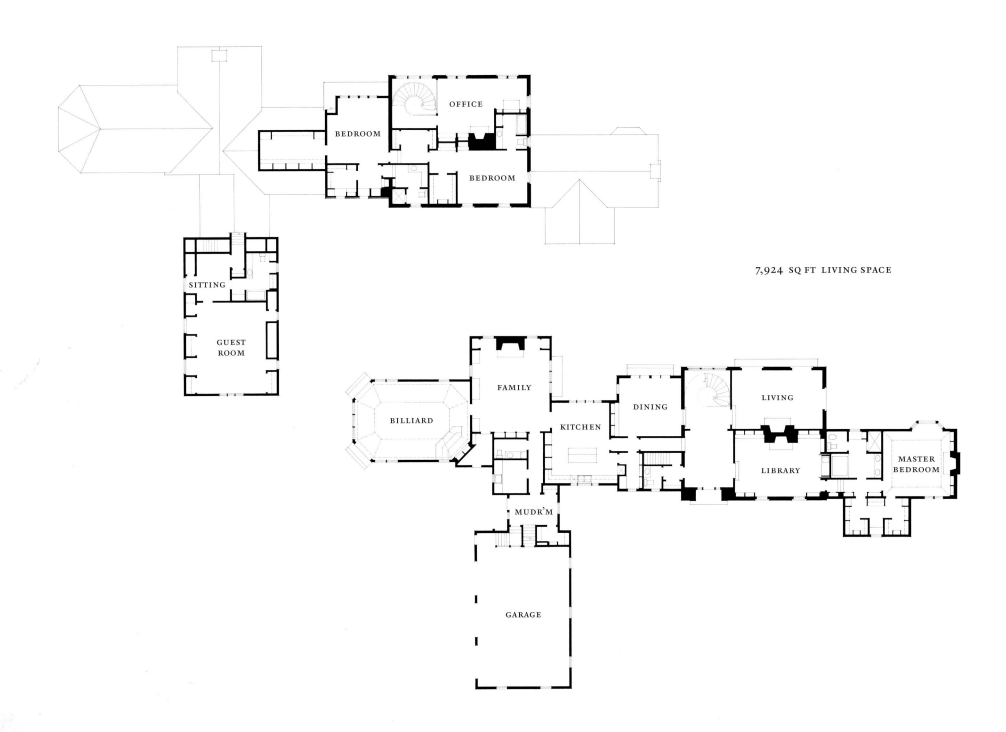

OFFICE

BEDROOM

BEDROOM

7,924 SQ FT LIVING SPACE

SITTING

GUEST ROOM

FAMILY

BILLIARD

KITCHEN

DINING

LIVING

LIBRARY

MASTER BEDROOM

MUDR'M

GARAGE

House on Cape Cod

The owners of this spectacular waterfront site on Cape Cod specifically requested a house in the "shingle style." The choice was appropriate not just because it allows a looser arrangement of living spaces well suited to a waterfront-activated lifestyle, but also because it allows a relatively compact building footprint, which was important for this particular site. The resulting design features the characteristic confection of overlapping, variably pitched dormers and gables, a number of oval windows, and the extruded edges of octagonal rooms and towers, the most notable of which is the cantilevered two-story glass stair hall adjacent to the front entry.

The romantic theme of the exterior has been carried over into the detailing of the interiors, which enjoy spectacular light reflected from the water. The full-length porch on the ground floor is a carefully considered way to control the intensity of that light while also allowing the ground-floor rooms to spill out toward the water.

The house is defined by a series of bays and multisided rooms that create intriguing spaces throughout the house.

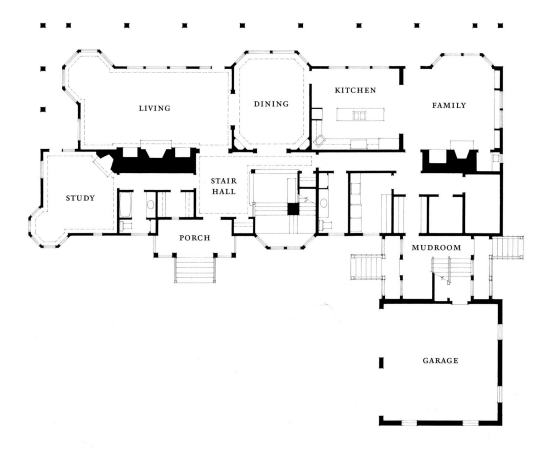

DECK

MASTER BEDROOM

BEDROOM

BEDROOM

DECK

LIVING

DINING

KITCHEN

FAMILY

STUDY

STAIR HALL

PORCH

MUDROOM

GARAGE

5,154 SQ FT LIVING SPACE

House in Falmouth

FALMOUTH, MASSACHUSETTS

This Colonial-inspired house in Falmouth, Massachusetts, is a classic design in virtually every sense of that word. Its composition, unified with the use of painted brick and clapboard, carefully and intentionally reinforces an overall impression of formality, reflecting the owner's specifications and lifestyle. It was designed and constructed at a time when Royal Barry Wills was in the process of handing over responsibilities to his successors, and the quality of its execution perfectly reflects the soundness of that transition.

The floor plan belies its age and is remarkable for the livability it suggests even today. The "snack room" off the kitchen portends the soon-to-be-ubiquitous family room, and the upstairs bedroom wing lends itself to use either for its originally intended accommodation of live-in help or to the needs of a contemporary family with children.

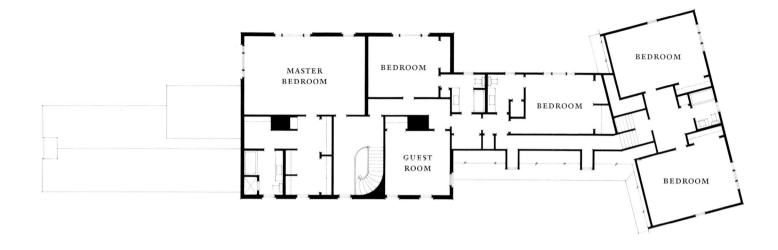

MASTER BEDROOM

BEDROOM

BEDROOM

BEDROOM

BEDROOM

GUEST ROOM

Compared to the home on the preceding pages, this plan demonstrates how living patterns were undergoing important changes. The snack room provides an informal gathering space for the family. The kitchen assumes a more open quality, and the bedrooms are more generously sized.

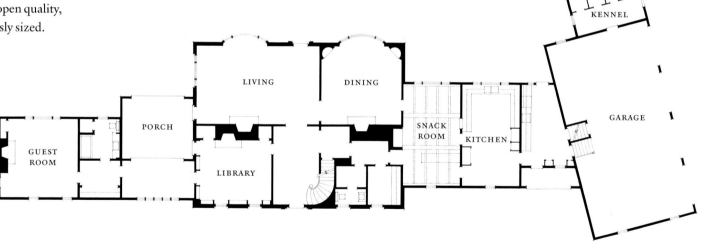

GUEST ROOM

PORCH

LIVING

DINING

LIBRARY

SNACK ROOM

KITCHEN

KENNEL

GARAGE

6,786 SQ FT LIVING SPACE

House in Oyster Harbors

OYSTER HARBORS, MASSACHUSETTS

The plan and organization of this house centers around a great room that here accommodates the functions of formal living and dining in a singular space. Given ample light by being pushed out the back of the house to expose its walls to the garden, this room retains a needed sense of formality by the way in which it is separated from the master bedroom suite and the study. It is a plan that reveals a careful attention to the aspirations of its owners, and to the way that they desired to live within it.

Unable to turn its doors away from the entry court, here the garage becomes a welcome addition to the composition through the use of a time-honored device; a simple three-point ellipse to frame the door openings dramatically softens the blow that would have come from the use of much more conventional, stark rectangular openings.

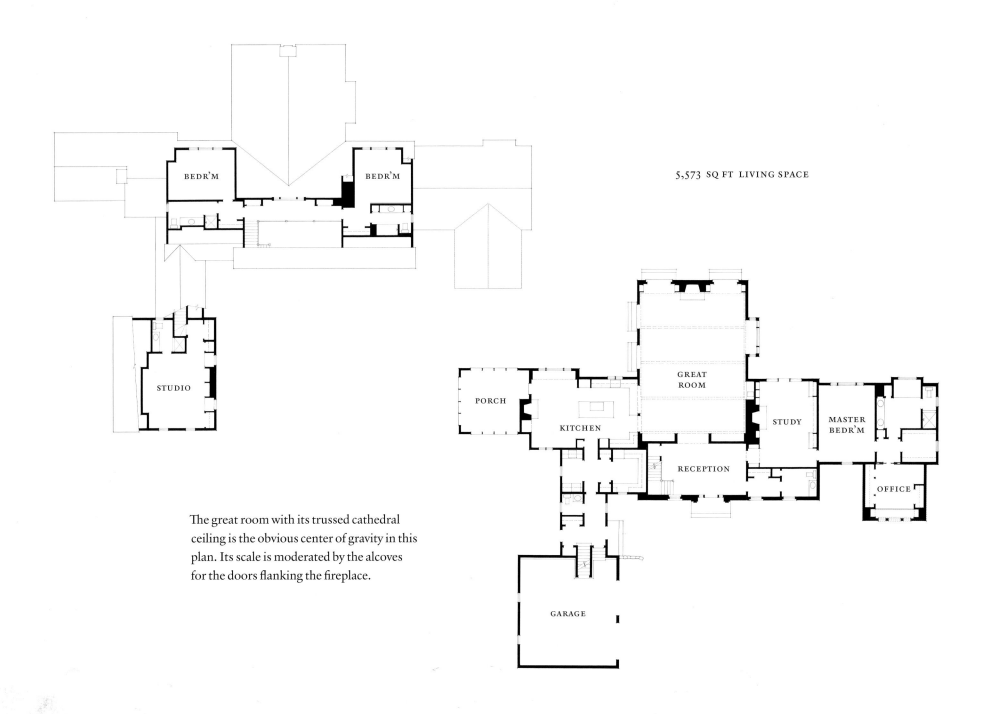

BEDR'M

BEDR'M

5,573 SQ FT LIVING SPACE

STUDIO

GREAT
ROOM

PORCH

STUDY

MASTER
BEDR'M

KITCHEN

RECEPTION

OFFICE

The great room with its trussed cathedral
ceiling is the obvious center of gravity in this
plan. Its scale is moderated by the alcoves
for the doors flanking the fireplace.

GARAGE

House in Little Compton

Crafting the correct scale—the relationship of parts to the whole—is an elusive yet indispensable quality in the creation of architecture. Of the many tools in the architect's tool box, it is also one of the most sophisticated at his or her disposal. This house in Little Compton is an essay in how the combination of different volumes, details, and geometry can establish a composition that encourages the eye, and with it the mind, to linger and inquire. Is it a large house made small, or a large house made more intimate? The small dormers and the extended arm of the garage with its covered connection back to the main house all act to accentuate the scale of the central block. Yet the larger size of the windows in the ancillary pieces provides a different perspective that challenges the impression of the size of the entire ensemble.

The materials used to add detail to the picture are local and traditional. The recessed front entrance is a prudent and time-tested response to seasonally inclement weather. And New England has an abundance of different types of stone—its miles of stacked stone walls are a regional treasure—that are ideally suited for veneers, chimneys, and landscaping. Here, too, the pieces used for the main wall of the house front figure in the conversation on scale both in their size and in the way they complement the weathered shingles used to clad the remainder of the house.

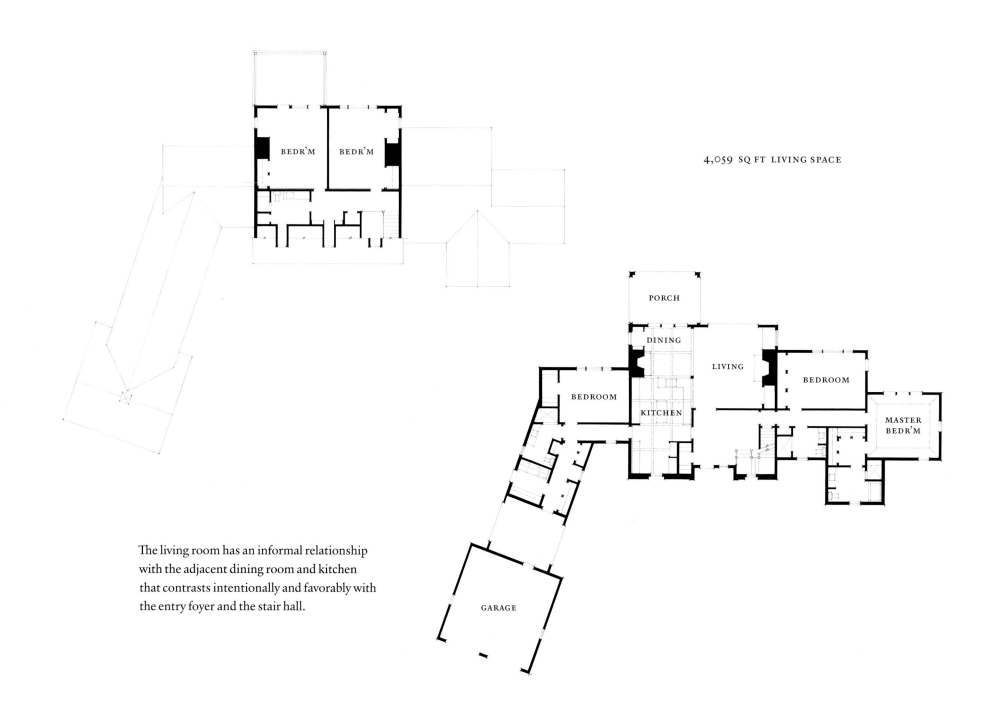

BEDR'M

BEDR'M

4,059 SQ FT LIVING SPACE

PORCH

DINING

LIVING

BEDROOM

KITCHEN

BEDROOM

MASTER
BEDR'M

The living room has an informal relationship
with the adjacent dining room and kitchen
that contrasts intentionally and favorably with
the entry foyer and the stair hall.

GARAGE

House in Osterville

A renovation of an existing house always poses certain challenges—will the new fit with the old, will it all add up to something greater than the individual parts—but when the subject is an older Royal Barry Wills house the stakes were even higher. The success of this project owes in large part to the general flexibility of the Colonial idiom.

The seductive waterfront site allows intimate contact with the calm watercourse, and the original design responded in a suitably informal way to frame it. Richard deftly used the garage, with its doors turned away from the entry drive, to give the house enough presence to hold the site without overpowering it, but also provided a logical path for its potential future expansion.

Over fifty years on, the value of this approach, and of a structure that can easily accommodate improvements, has been well proven. The new pieces, including a kitchen, outdoor porch, and the master bedroom wing are somewhat grander than their kin, but that seems easily justified by the value the earlier decisions have created. The comprehensive approach to the renovation of the entire interior has ensured that the new house not only reflects the tastes and interests of its owners, but also that the new rooms blend seamlessly with the originals.

The plan is laid out to give all major rooms a view of the cove and neighboring marsh. The kitchen, porch, and master bedroom were the main areas that benefitted from expansion.

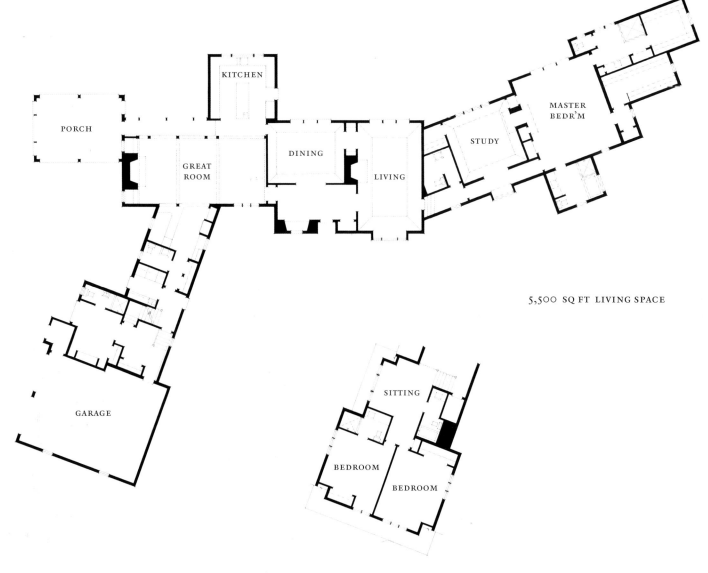

KITCHEN

PORCH

GREAT ROOM

DINING

LIVING

STUDY

MASTER BEDR'M

5,500 SQ FT LIVING SPACE

GARAGE

SITTING

BEDROOM

BEDROOM

The sun porch adopts a bolder architectural >
vocabulary but still matches the scale and
materials of the main house.

With any renovation, interiors take
on a different character that reflects
the particular tastes of the owner.

The four-season "porch" has a commanding   >
view of the garden and the pond beyond.

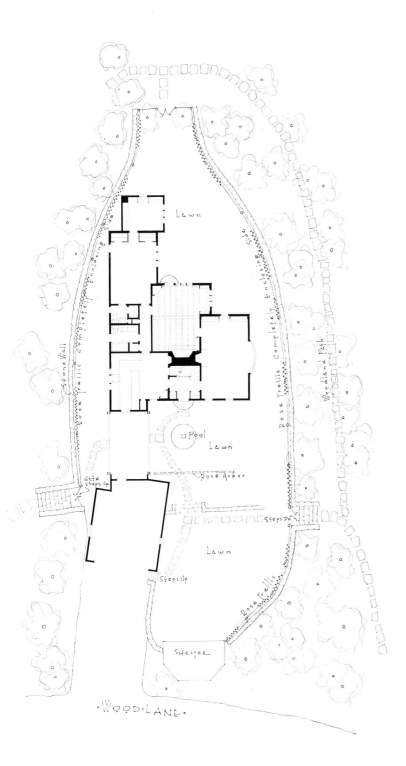

House in Winchester

WINCHESTER, MASSACHUSETTS

R oyal Barry Wills enjoyed a challenge, and when an opportunity arose for him to design a house for himself, he managed to find the most challenging site possible in this Boston suburb. Designing a house to be built within the walls of an existing landscaped rose garden with minimum disruption faced him here. One cut in the wall for the garage entrance and the removal of one arched trellis gave him the space to deftly plan a house that slipped in and around the existing landscaping.

Royal liked to use old and reclaimed building materials. The arches from the rose trellis now form the arches for the screened porch. Old cypress clapboards are used for siding along with reclaimed barn boards. A foray to a building wrecking yard produced doors, pine boards, paneling, beams, and bricks for the interior.

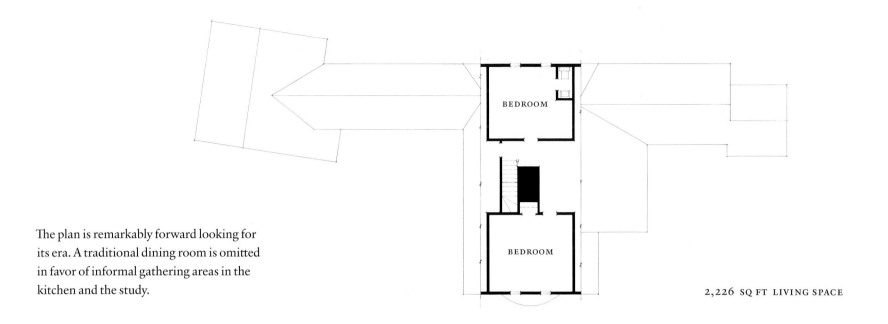

The plan is remarkably forward looking for its era. A traditional dining room is omitted in favor of informal gathering areas in the kitchen and the study.

2,226 SQ FT LIVING SPACE

The study features a walk-in fireplace >
and hand-hewn beam ceiling that could
have been transported directly from
the eighteenth century.

The entrance plank door has pilasters and
a transom rescued from the scrap pile.

< The living room paneled wall
   was reclaimed from a house long
   gone by the wrecking ball.

Royal Barry Wills

Marguerite Wills and Royal Barry Wills >
at home, circa 1957.

STAFF, CIRCA 1958: Merton S. Barrows,
Robert E. Minot, Royal Barry Wills,
Richard Wills, Warren J. Rohter

CURRENT STAFF: G. Alexander Domenico,
Todd T. Fix, Richard Wills, David Stuhlsatz,
(not pictured, Lynn J. Talacko from the
Maine office)

Notes

1. Arnold Nicholson, "Big Man in Small Houses," *Saturday Evening Post*, March 29, 1958.
2. Richard Guy Wilson, *The Colonial Revival House* (New York: Abrams, 2004), 6.
3. Nicholson, "Big Man in Small Houses."
4. Nicholson, "Big Man in Small Houses."
5. David Gebhard, "Royal Barry Wills and the American Colonial Revival," *Winterthur Portfolio* 27, no. 1 (1992). Noted historian Gebhard is one of the few scholars to have examined the deserving but too little explored story of this enormously influential architect and his times.
6. Gebhard, "Royal Barry Wills."
7. Gebhard, "Royal Barry Wills."
8. Royal Barry Wills, *This Business of Architecture* (New York: Reinhold Publishing, 1941), 34, 55.
9. Wills, *This Business of Architecture*, 34, 36.
10. Wills, *This Business of Architecture*, 38.
11. Gebhard, "Royal Barry Wills."
12. Letters to the Editor, *Life*, September 16, 1946.
13. Gebhard, "Royal Barry Wills."
14. "Royal Barry Wills: Boston Architect Designs the Kinds of Houses Most Americans Want, *Life*, August 26, 1946, 67.
15. Nicholson, "Big Man in Small Houses."
16. Andrew Shanken, *194X: Architecture, Planning, and Consumer Culture on the American Home Front* (Minneapolis: University of Minnesota Press, 2009), 4.
17. Shanken, *194X*, 4.
18. Dolores Hayden, *Building Suburbia: Green Fields and Urban Growth 1820–2000* (New York: Vintage, 2003), 131.
19. Hayden, *Building Suburbia*, 132.
20. Gebhard, "Royal Barry Wills," 57.
21. "The New England Tradition and Royal Barry Wills, a New England Primer," *House & Home*, February 1960.

Image Credits

Todd Fix, front and back covers, 2, 6, 8, 11, 12, 20, 32, 35, 36, 36–37, 38, 39, 40–41, 41, 43, 44, 47, 54, 55, 57, 58–59, 59, 70, 71, 73, 74, 74–75, 76, 79, 80, 81, 83, 84, 87, 89, 90, 93 all, 98, 99, 101, 102–103, 103, 104, 105, 107, 108 all, 109, 110, 111, 113, 114, 115, 120, 121, 123, 124, 127, 128 left, 129, 130, 131, 133 left & bottom right, 134, 135, 137, 138, 139 all, 141, 143, 150, 151, 153, 158, 166, 170, 173, 174, 175 all, 176, 177, 179, 181; 190 right; Sara Gray, 4, 48, 51, 52 all, 53; Robert Keller, 21; Ken Duprey, 61, 63 all, 64, 65, 116, 117, 119 all, 162, 163, 165, 190 left; Patrick Wiseman, 66, 67 all, 69; Mark Cote, 77; Arthur C. Haskell, 85, 88, 182; Robert J. Schellhammer, 94, 95, 97; Paul Maue Associates, 128 right; unknown, 133 top right, 157, 189; Douglas R. Gilbert, 140, 154, 155 all, 159 all, 161, 167, 169; Steve Vierra, 144, 147, 148 all, 148–149; Michael Partenio, 180 all; Zaharis, Ipswich, MA, 185; Lisanti Inc., NY, NY, 186, 187, 188

Published by Rowman & Littlefield
4501 Forbes Boulevard, Suite 200, Lanham, Maryland 20706
www.rowman.com

10 Thornbury Road, Plymouth PL6 7PP, United Kingdom

Distributed by National Book Network

British Library Cataloguing in Publication Information Available

LIBRARY OF CONGRESS CATALOGING-IN-PUBLICATION DATA
Wills, Richard, 1926–
    At Home in New England : Royal Barry Wills Architects 1925 to Present /
Richard Wills with Keith Orlesky.
        pages cm
    Includes bibliographical references.
    ISBN 978-1-4422-2425-4 (cloth : alk. paper) — ISBN 978-1-4422-2426-1
(electronic : alk. paper) 1. Royal Barry Wills Associates. 2. Architecture, Domestic—New England. I. Title.
    NA737.R69A4 2013
    728.092'2—dc23
2013014866

Book design by Julia Sedykh with Todd Fix

Manufactured in China